Old World Breads!

Charel Scheele

OLD WORLD BREADS

iUniverse books may be ordered through booksellers or by contacting:

iUniverse
1663 Liberty Drive
Bloomington, IN 47403
www.iuniverse.com
844-349-9409

Originally published by The Crossing Press Specialty Cookbook Series

ISBN: 978-1-4697-0655-9 (sc)

Print information available on the last page.

iUniverse rev. date: 10/06/2020

Contents

To my wife, Ingrid, whose help made this book possible

Preface

ⲟⲟⲟ

*Wars are fought
And prayers said
For food so simple
As a loaf of bread*

In Europe every locality has its own bread. These recipes were based in part on the grains available. Some soils were better for wheat growing, others for rye. The climate played a role in the quality of the grain. Without modern transportation and communication, the bakers in each region perfected their own bread recipes, and these became typical of the area with the passing of time.

European breads are usually crustier, heartier, and have more subtle flavor differences than American breads. They are made with fresher ingredients, which give them a nuttier flavor; they are baked more often so they are fresher; and they are baked on baking sheets rather than in bread pans, which contributes to the crusty exterior and allows the breads to be shaped into the characteristic round and oblong loaves.

Another difference: Most European bakers use a different recipe for each type of bread. In the U.S., where we tend to simplify everything to save time, most bakers adapt just two or three basic recipes to make a whole array of different products. With mass production, flavor and quality are often sacrificed, and the texture frequently has a rubbery quality. Often the fragrant, subtle flavors, which are still found in European breads, are lost in American baking.

However, the making of tasty homemade bread is happily enjoying one of its biggest revivals in America. And every year more and more people travel to Europe and taste the delicious European breads.

As a professional baker at one time and another on both continents, I would like to share with you some of my knowledge of bread baking. If you already are an experienced baker, you will find a good variety of recipes to add to your repertoire. If you are a novice, you will find these recipes easy to follow and almost foolproof.

I grew up in a family of bakers, a trade which

by European tradition is passed on from father to son for generations. My grandfather started with one bakery in the small city of Axel, in the Dutch part of Flanders, about two miles from the Belgian border. The bakery consisted of two brick buildings attached to a store and a three-story house.

I was a child when electricity was first installed in the bakery. Originally, all the work was done by hand. Light came from an oil lamp, and so the place was always dimly lit, except when someone opened the heavy cast iron door of the brick oven—then the fire would light up everything for a few moments.

There was no heating system in the old bakery. On cold wintry days, the place was kept comfortable with the heat coming from the wood-fired brick oven. In the summer, the top half of the Dutch door and the small windows were kept open for ventilation.

Before and after school, I worked at the bakery. One of my most satisfying jobs in the winter was to build a great big wood fire in the baking chamber of the oven, which could handle as many as two hundred loaves of bread at one time. It was loaded three or four times a day. A small fire was made between loads of bread to reheat the oven.

It was more than satisfying to take the fresh loaves of golden brown bread out of the oven with a long-handled paddle. No bread pans were used; a little cornmeal or bran was sprinkled on the oven floor to keep the dough from sticking.

In the old days, white, rye, and whole wheat breads were baked daily. Other breads were baked only once a week. For instance, on Tuesdays we baked barley bread, and this bread became known as Tuesday's Bread. On Fridays we baked a bran bread. Because bran cost less than wheat flour, the bread was priced a few cents less than the other breads. Many of the working people bought this bread, and so it became known as Workman's Bread. Sweet breads, special breads, and raisin breads were usually baked for Sundays and holidays.

As soon as the first batch of bread was ready each day, my grandfather would open the top half of the Dutch door and blow a copper horn. This was the signal that fresh baked bread was available. The pleasing odor of the still-warm loaves permeated the store, the house, and spread out into the street. Soon people came from all over to buy their bread. Although some bread was delivered by bicycle to neighboring areas, most was sold right over the counter. No loaf was wrapped or sliced, the customers came with their own bread baskets, huge affairs with handles that could be carried on the arm.

When people came to the bakery for their bread, they generally were happy to stay and chat. So the bakery also became a center of news in the neighborhood. The customers knew each other and would share their happy events and sad stories. They cared for one another and often would help out in times of need. That friendliness contributed to the atmosphere of the bakery in those olden days.

My grandfather's bakery is still in existence today, but it is no longer a family operation. With the passing of time it has been modernized. The old brick oven was replaced with a modern electric one. The oil lamp was replaced with electric lights, and the wooden mixing trough with modern machinery.

After I finished regular schooling, I attended a special school for bread bakers. Later I went to another school for pastries. At one time I worked for five years as a professional baker in New York City. But mostly I have baked as a hobby and have won many ribbons for the breads I have entered in local and state fairs in Wyoming. I have traveled extensively throughout the world and collected recipes from different places. Many of these I have adapted to suit the American kitchen.

As you start making your own bread, begin by selecting high-quality ingredients for the best flavor. The difference in taste becomes very apparent as you get used to eating good bread. For example, if you have to choose between using sugar or honey, choose honey. Honey not only gives bread a fine flavor but it keeps your bread fresh longer and it greatly improves its keeping quality. Although honey might cost a few pennies more than sugar, these pennies are well spent. Also, do use a good quality oil instead of shortening. And don't forget that sour milk and leftover potato water make fine bread.

You don't have to live on a farm to enjoy good bread. Your efforts in baking bread will be rewarded by everyone's pleasure as they sink their teeth into your fine homemade bread. This is bread that is not only delicious, it is also very nutritious.

1
Bread Making Basics

There was a time when one could call all bread the staff of life. Bread in those good old days was made of a variety of nutritious ingredients right in the home kitchen. But all that changed around the turn of the century as the use of more modern machinery helped to move the baking of bread out of the home and into the bread factories.

However, all is not lost. Making homemade breads is not as difficult as it may sound. You can start with a plain white or light wheat bread. This gives you the opportunity to get some experience and to get to know your oven. After some experience behind you, you can tackle sweet breads and then sourdough breads.

In general you should follow the recipes closely and use exactly the amount of ingredients indicated in the recipe. But because of the weather and conditions of storage, the amount of flour needed to make a dough might vary slightly.

It is helpful to become familiar with the ingredients used most in bread making: flour, yeast, fats and oils, eggs, and sweeteners.

Flour. Flour is marketed in several forms. Much of today's white flour is bleached. This allows the miller to use an inferior grain and bleach it to give it a white appearance. Whenever white flour is called for, we use only all-purpose unbleached flour in our recipes to insure quality.

Whole wheat flour or graham flour is milled from the whole kernel. Because it contains all the natural oils found in the wheat germ, it should be stored in a cool place to prevent rancidity.

Bran is the outer layer of the wheat kernel. It adds fiber to your bread, but it also makes it heavier, so use it only in the quantities indicated.

Rye flour is a favorite in European breads. It's always mixed with white or whole wheat flour in bread recipes. There are two types of rye flour available: dark and light. Both are excellent for different kinds of breads.

Pumpernickel is another name for rye meal. It is ground coarser than rye flour and it is also favored by Europeans. In our area, pumpernickel is easily available in the supermarkets. You may find it in health food stores or in European ethnic stores.

Buckwheat flour gives a very distinctive flavor to bread. It is found in some supermarkets and in natural food stores.

Rolled oats will give a moist, soft texture to bread.

Barley flour makes a flavorful bread. You may find it in some supermarkets and in most health food stores.

Yeast. Yeast comes in two forms: dry and compressed. In Europe most bakers use fresh compressed yeast. They contend that fresh yeast gives bread a better texture, a lighter density, and even a better flavor. The differences are very subtle. If you cannot find fresh compressed yeast, you can easily substitute the dry kind. One level tablespoon of dry yeast is equivalent to one cake of compressed yeast. Both kinds are found in many supermarkets. The fresh yeast is mostly found in the dairy case or other refrigerated area of the supermarkets. Both compressed yeast and dry yeast are marked with expiration dates; before starting a recipe, make sure your yeast is not past its expiration date.

Fats and Oils. The purpose of fats and oils is to tenderize the dough. We prefer to use oil over butter or another solid shortening because the particles of a good oil will distribute more evenly in the dough. In America I have adapted to the use of corn oil as I find it a little sweeter than other vegetable oils, but this is a personal preference. Any good vegetable oil can be used in the place of corn oil. Olive oil can be used where you want a strong flavor, but its use isn't advised in most breads.

Eggs. Eggs act as a leavening agent. They also add color and flavor to the baked product.

Sweeteners. Sweeteners add flavor and increase tenderness. They also help to brown the crust. We prefer to use honey in most breads, as honey helps to keep bread fresh and soft longer. I also have a personal preference for sorghum. Sorghum is a syrup made from the juices of the cereal grass or plant with the same name. Sorghum is grown in Africa, South America, around the Mediterranean, and in southern U.S. The syrup looks a little like molasses, but it is sweeter and lacks the strong, bitter taste of molasses. You can substitute honey or sugar for sorghum in equal measure. Do not substitute molasses for sorghum, except in rye breads, because molasses will give a bitter taste to bread.

A Note on Salt. Salt enhances the flavor of bread, but it is damaging to the yeast. You will notice that in most of my recipes salt comes toward the end of the ingredients list. This is because you want the salt as far away from the yeast as possible when you add the ingredients to the mixing bowl. I usually add the salt to the flour before mixing all the ingredients together.

Basic Bread Making Steps

1. Assembling the Ingredients. Always have all tools and all ingredients at room temperature. Never use cold flour or eggs out of the refrigerator. The cold will hamper the rising of the dough.

2. Dissolving the Yeast. Always dissolve the yeast in liquid that is between 105° F. and 115° F. Yeast is alive and will not work right when temperatures are too low or too high. Do not use yeast that is past the expiration date marked on its package.

3. Mixing. The purpose of mixing is to blend all the ingredients so as to stretch the gluten. Gluten is a protein naturally found in some grains. It is activated by mixing the flour with liquids. The gluten forms the structure of the breads, holding the carbon dioxide that is released by the yeast. This makes your bread light and tasty.

The mixing can be done by hand, with a wooden spoon, or with an electric mixer, as long as the mixing is thorough. Unless you use a dough hook with your electric mixer, you will have to stir in the final cup or so of flour by hand.

The approximate amount of flour you will need is given in each recipe. Due to the weather and where the flour was stored, the amount may vary slightly. Start with half the amount, or less. Then, as you mix, add the rest of the flour in small amounts, maybe one cup at a time. Reserve at least 1/3 cup of flour to be used in kneading.

The mixture will get thick and heavy and begin to feel like a soft pliable dough. It is ready for kneading when you can no longer mix in flour.

4. Kneading. Turn the dough out onto a lightly floured surface, such as a kitchen counter top. Fold the dough over toward you and push down forward with the heel of both hands. Now, give the dough a quarter turn and repeat the motion, folding the dough toward you and pushing down with the heel of your hands. Repeat this motion until the dough is smooth. It will have a good elastic feel and look somewhat glossy. This will take about 6 minutes. If the dough seems too soft and sticky, add a little more flour and knead it until it is smooth and elastic.

For a real crusty bread you can start the kneading process by punching and stretching. By stretching the dough and drawing it out and then punching it, you will develop the gluten somewhat differently, and the result will be a light crusty bread. Punch and stretch for 1 to 2 minutes only. Then finish kneading the dough as described above. This punch and stretch method should not be used for rich sweet doughs.

When you have finished kneading, form the dough into a round ball and put it back into the mixing bowl. Some people like to grease the bowl. I never found it necessary. Cover it with a clean towel and let the dough rise.

5. Rising. This gives dough a rest so the yeast can work. To get a fine texture always keep the dough in a warm place, at about 80° F., free from drafts. In the winter you can make a good place for the dough to rise by placing the covered bowl on the top rack in a cold oven; on the lower rack, set a bowl or pan of hot water. Close the oven door.

Rising usually takes from 45 to 60 minutes. The rising times given are approximate, depending on the outside temperatures. In winter it will take a few minutes longer than in the summer. The dough should about double in bulk. To tell if the dough is ready, lightly press two fingertips about 1/4 inch into dough. If the dough does not hold the slight indentation your fingers made, it is not ready. If the indentation remains, the dough is ready for the next step, which is shaping.

6. Shaping the Dough. Most of the recipes make two loaves. So divide the dough in two equal parts on a lightly floured surface. Let the dough rest for approximately 10 minutes.

To make a regular loaf shape, flatten the dough with the palm of your hand into a rectangle measuring 16 x 10 inches. Fold one side over, then fold the other side over, overlapping by about 1 inch. Press flat again, then tightly roll into a loaf. Set on a prepared baking sheet or in a greased loaf pan, seam side down. If you feel creative you can score the top of the loaves with 5 or 6 diagonal slashes, or with just one shallow horizontal cut along the center of the loaf, or with slashes in a zig-zag pattern. Use a very sharp knife.

To make a round loaf, shape the dough into a ball. The best way to do this is to lightly flour your hands and use both hands to make a round ball. Flatten this ball slightly before you put it onto a baking sheet. If you like, you can score the top of the loaf. I seldom do so.

To make a braid, divide the dough into 3 parts. Roll each of these parts into a rope about 18 inches long. Put the 3 ropes alongside each other with

1 inch of space between each. Interweave the ropes into a loose braid. Pinch the ends together firmly. Set the braids onto baking sheets.

To make a braided ring, bring both outer points of the braid together to form a ring. Pinch the ends together firmly. Set them on the prepared baking sheets as a ring.

7. Setting the Loaves onto the Baking Sheet. Always grease the baking sheet or generously sprinkle it with cornmeal. To grease the baking sheet, I prefer to use a vegetable shortening. If you use oil and bake frequently, the baking sheet eventually will become sticky and hard to clean. Butter and margarine burn too easily. I've found that vegetable shortening works the best, doesn't affect the bread, and is easier to clean afterwards.

Cover the loaves with a clean towel after you've set them on the baking sheets. Let them rise again for the approximate time indicated in the recipes.

You can use greased bread loaf pans for all the recipes, but a baking sheet will give you more of an European bread.

Note: If you plan to bake your bread in a brick oven (see page 15), let the bread rise on your kitchen counter, which should be first dusted with cornmeal.

8. Baking the Loaves. Preheat the oven for 5 minutes to the temperature desired. Bake the loaves as indicated in the recipe, usually from 30 to 60 minutes. When done, the loaves should sound somewhat hollow when you tap them with your fingers. If you have used a bread pan, the loaves should shrink a little from the sides of the bread pan when done.

If the bread browns too quickly, cover each loaf with aluminum foil as it bakes.

9. Cooling. After baking, remove the bread from the pan or baking sheet at once. Place the loaves on a wire rack to cool. A wire rack will let the air circulate freely around the loaves, preventing them from losing their crustiness.

To let the flavor mature, cool each loaf for about 1 hour before eating it. This will also allow the loaf to firm so that it can be sliced without tearing—that is, if you can keep your family's hands off until it has cooled down sufficiently. Serve fresh.

10. Storing bread. If you like crusty, good tasting bread, do not wrap it. French bakers stand their loaves on one end so that cool air can freely circulate around them. Bread that has been wrapped loses its crustiness. Most Europeans eat bread that has never been wrapped. They bake every day or at least every other day. If you plan to keep your bread for more than two days, however, it is necessary to put each loaf into a plastic bag. Do so only after it has thoroughly cooled. Then store it in a cool, dry place. If you like a soft crust, cover the loaves with a towel while cooling.

We like our breads crusty, so in our house we bake three times a week and never wrap or cover the loaves.

Bread can be kept in the freezer for several weeks. To store in the freezer, wrap the bread after it has cooled thoroughly. Use a moisture-proof material such as a plastic wrap, and make it airtight. To serve, thaw the bread at room temperature for several hours. Then use it quickly.

Sponge Method

The purpose of the sponge method is to make a crustier, tastier bread. This is accomplished by mixing part of the liquid, yeast, and flour together and letting them ferment for 1/2 hour to 3 1/2 hours.

Any sponge that ferments for 5 hours or more is properly called a sourdough, because after 5 hours, the flour, yeast, and water begin to sour.

Creating a Brick Oven Effect In Your Kitchen

To create a brick oven effect in your kitchen, you will need a red clay flower pot saucer (not the flower pot—just the saucer).

In an old-fashioned brick oven, only the bottom of the bread makes contact with the hot bricks. To imitate this effect, use a red clay saucer that is bigger than your one round loaf of bread so that the sides of the dough do not touch the sides of the saucer. Only the bottom of the round loaf should make contact with the hot red clay. A twelve-inch-diameter red clay saucer will be big enough for any recipe that uses 6 cups of flour or less. Do not use a glazed clay dish, because then you will lose the brick oven effect.

To prepare a red clay saucer for bread baking, first wash the saucer clean. Let it dry thoroughly. Then grease the inside of the saucer with vegetable shortening. Vegetable shortening will spread and be absorbed more evenly than oil. Place the empty saucer in a cold oven. Turn the oven to 250° F. Bake the saucer for 20 minutes. Then increase the oven temperature to 350° F. Bake for another 20 minutes. Finally increase the oven temperature to 450° F. Bake for 20 minutes. Turn the oven off but leave the saucer in the oven for 2 hours to cool slowly. After the saucer has cooled, scrub it with hot water (do not use soap). Now you will not need to grease the red clay saucer again when baking bread in it. If you do grease it again, it will not stay porous and you will lose the brick oven effect.

Before each use, put the empty saucer in a cold oven 10 minutes before baking. Preheat the oven to 400° F. with the empty saucer in it. When the oven has reached 400° F., carefully remove the piping hot saucer, liberally sprinkle it with cornmeal and place your round loaf in it. It is easier if you use a baker's peel or paddle to move the loaf. But I've done it innumerable times without a peel. I just use both hands and transfer the loaf very gently into the hot saucer, being careful not to handle it roughly. Carefully return the saucer with the loaf in it to the oven and bake until the bread is golden brown. The porous red clay retains the heat just like the bricks in a brick oven and produces a delicious golden crust.

Common Mistakes in Bread Making

As with any human endeavor, things do go wrong occasionally. But do not despair. Sometimes even a so-called bad loaf of homemade bread is better than a store-bought one. Find out what went wrong and use this knowledge to make a better loaf next time. Here are some suggestions to avoid the most common mistakes that occur in bread baking.

A) Dough rose too little or not at all:
 1) The liquid in which you dissolved the yeast was too hot—over 115° F.
 2) The ingredients were stored in refrigerator and not allowed to come to room temperature. This made the dough too cold.
 3) The yeast was too old.
 4) The dough was set to rise in a cold and/or drafty place.

B) Crust too hard:
 1) Congratulations—Europeans love a hard crust.
 2) The oven was too hot.
 3) The dough was too stiff. Use less flour next time.
 4) The next time cover the loaves with a clean towel as they cool on the wire rack. This will soften the crust.

C) Bread is sticky or soggy in the middle:
 1) The bread was not baked long enough.
 2) The oven temperature was too low.

3) The dough didn't rise long enough after it was shaped.

D) Bread crust too dark:
1) The oven was too hot.

E) Uneven rising:
1) The dough was shaped incorrectly.
2) The oven was too full—too many loaves in the oven.
3) The dough was kept in a drafty place.
4) The loaves were put too close to the oven walls.

F) Bread falls or collapses in the oven:
1) The dough rose too long.
2) You opened the oven door during baking.
3) An earthquake occurred during baking.

G) Bread has big holes:
1) The dough rose too long.
2) Too much yeast was used.
3) Insufficient kneading.

H) The loaves spread out and did not rise as they should have on the baking sheets:
1) Not enough flour was used.
2) The loaves were not rolled tightly enough.

2
White Breads

oooooooooooooooooooooooooooooooooooooooooooooooooooooooooooooooooooooooooooooooo

Vienna-Style Bread

One of the most pleasant traditions in Vienna in the summer is the tasting of the new wine made from the grapes of the previous autumn. Wine growers set out long tables, often under trees. Usually a light white wine is served with smoked meats, cheeses, radishes, and some good Vienna-style bread.

1 cake yeast
1 cup warm (110° F.) water
Approximately 6 cups unbleached
   all-purpose flour
1 cup warm (110° F.) milk
1 teaspoon corn oil or vegetable oil
1 teaspoon honey or sugar
2 egg whites, at room temperature,
   lightly beaten
1 teaspoon salt
Sesame seeds

Yield: 2 medium-size loaves

In a 6-quart mixing bowl, dissolve the yeast in the water. Add 1 cup of the flour. Mix well. Let this ferment for 1 hour in a warm (75° F.) place. Then add the milk, oil, honey, 1 of the egg whites, the salt, and the remaining 5 cups flour, working them into a dough.

Turn the dough out onto a lightly floured surface and knead it for 6 to 7 minutes, until the dough is smooth, elastic, and glossy.

Return the dough to the mixing bowl and cover it with a towel. Let rise in a warm (75° F.) place for 1 hour, or until doubled in bulk.

Divide the dough into 2 equal halves and shape each piece into an oblong loaf. Set the loaves on a baking sheet that has been liberally dusted with cornmeal. Brush with the remaining egg white and sprinkle with sesame seeds. Let rise again in a warm place for 45 to 50 minutes.

Bake in a preheated 400° F. oven for 30 to 35 minutes, or until golden brown. Remove from the baking sheet at once and cool on a wire rack. Serve warm.

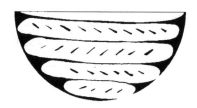

Challah

This delicious golden braid stays fresh for several days.

Bread

1 cake yeast
2 cups warm (110° F.) potato cooking water
1 tablespoon vegetable oil
1 tablespoon honey or sugar
2 eggs, at room temperature, lightly beaten
1 teaspoon pure vanilla extract
1 teaspoon salt
Approximately 6 cups unbleached
   all-purpose flour

Glaze

1 egg, at room temperature, lightly beaten
Poppy seeds

Yield: 2 small braids

In a 6-quart mixing bowl, dissolve the yeast in the potato cooking water. Add the remaining bread ingredients, mixing the salt with the flour, and work them into a dough.

Turn the dough onto a lightly floured surface and knead it for 6 to 7 minutes.

Return the dough to the mixing bowl and cover it with a towel. Let the dough rise in a warm (75° F.) place for 1 hour, or until doubled in bulk.

Divide the dough into 6 equal parts and roll each into a 12-inch rope. Braid 3 ropes together, and then braid the other 3, and set on a lightly greased baking sheet. Brush with the beaten egg and sprinkle with poppy seeds. Let rise again for 50 minutes.

Bake in a preheated 350° F. oven for 50 minutes, or until golden brown. Remove from the baking sheet at once and cool on a wire rack.

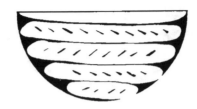

Crusty French Bread

Good bread and wine are serious business to the French. Who hasn't seen scenes in French movies where a man or a woman carry home long loaves of unwrapped bread sticking out of a shopping bag or strapped to the back of a bicycle? These crisp loaves—fluffy on the inside, crusty on the outside— are absolutely delicious with a Camembert or Brie cheese and a glass of good French wine.

1 cake fresh yeast
2 cups warm (110° F.) water
Approximately 5 1/2 to 6 cups unbleached all-purpose flour
2 egg whites, at room temperature, lightly beaten
1 teaspoon salt

Yield: 4 long loaves

In a 6-quart mixing bowl, dissolve half the yeast in 1 cup of the water. Add 1 cup of the flour. Mix well. Let this mixture ferment in a warm (75° F.) place for 3 1/2 hours. Then add the rest of the yeast and the water. Mix well. Add the remaining ingredients, including the remaining 4 1/2 to 5 cups flour, and work them into a dough.

Turn the dough out onto a lightly floured surface and knead it for 6 to 7 minutes, until the dough is smooth, elastic, and somewhat glossy. If you like, use the punch and stretch method described on page 12.

Return the dough to the mixing bowl and cover it with a towel. Let the dough rise in a warm (75° F.) place for 1 hour, or until doubled in bulk.

Divide the dough into 4 equal parts and shape each part into a long loaf. Set the loaves on 2 baking sheets that have been liberally dusted with cornmeal. Score the loaves with 3 or 4 diagonal slashes made with a sharp knife. Cover the loaves with a towel and let them rise again in a warm place for about 1 hour.

Bake in a preheated 400° F. oven for 30 minutes, or until golden brown. Remove the loaves from the baking sheets at once and allow them to cool on a wire rack.

Note: This bread is really crusty if baked as suggested. Some bakers like to spray the oven with water or have a pan of water in the oven as they bake this bread to make a crustier loaf, but I never found it necessary to do so in our oven. You can experiment with these methods to find out which you like the best.

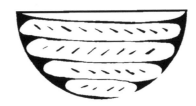

Crusty Soup Bread

Similar to the traditional French bread, this bread is a richer tasting sourdough, and the crust is not quite so brittle. The bread makes a perfect accompaniment to an old-fashioned Dutch iron kettle of soup or stew. It is also very good with Edam or Gouda cheese and wine.

1 cake yeast
2 cups warm (110° F.) water
Approximately 6 cups unbleached all-purpose
  flour
2 egg whites, at room temperature, lightly
  beaten
1 teaspoon vegetable oil
1 teaspoon sorghum or sugar
1 teaspoon salt
Sesame seeds

Yield: 6 small loaves

In a 6-quart mixing bowl, dissolve half the yeast in 1 cup water. Add 1 cup flour. Mix well. Ferment overnight in a warm (75° F.) place. Then add the rest of the yeast and the water. Mix well. Add 1 egg white, the oil, sorghum, salt, and remaining 5 cups flour and work into a dough.

Turn the dough out onto a lightly floured surface and knead it for 6 to 7 minutes, until the dough is smooth, elastic, and glossy.

Return the dough to the mixing bowl and cover with a towel. Let rise in a warm (75° F.) place for 1 hour, or until doubled in bulk.

Divide the dough into 6 equal parts and roll each into a cylindrical shape about 12 inches long. Set on baking sheets that have been liberally dusted with cornmeal. Brush with the remaining egg white and sprinkle with sesame seeds. Let rise again in a warm place for 50 to 60 minutes.

Bake in a preheated 400° F. oven for 10 minutes. Then reduce the oven to 375° F. and bake for 20 minutes. Remove from the baking sheets and cool on a wire rack.

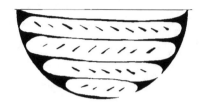

Italian Bread

This interesting recipe comes from northern Italy. Instead of the usual pure white Italian loaf, this bread is slightly red in color from the tomato juice. The flavor is subtle and can be enhanced with the addition of a little dill seed.

1 cake yeast
1 cup warm (110° F.) water
Approximately 6 cups unbleached all-purpose
   flour
1 cup warm (110° F.) tomato juice
1 teaspoon vegetable oil
2 egg whites, at room temperature,
   lightly beaten
1 teaspoon salt

Yield: 3 long loaves

In a 6-quart mixing bowl, dissolve the yeast in the water. Add 1 cup of the flour. Mix well. Let this mixture stand for 30 minutes. Then add the tomato juice and all the other ingredients, and work them into a dough.

Turn the dough out onto a lightly floured surface and knead it for 6 to 7 minutes.

Return the dough to the mixing bowl and cover it with a towel. Let the dough rise in a warm (75° F.) place for 1 hour, or until doubled in bulk.

Divide the dough into 3 equal parts and shape each part into a long loaf. Set the loaves on a large baking sheet that has been liberally dusted with cornmeal. Cover the loaves with a towel and let them rise again in a warm place for 50 minutes.

Bake in a preheated 400° F. oven for 35 minutes. Remove the loaves from the baking sheet at once and cool on a wire rack.

Post-War White Bread

During World War II, food was in short supply in many nations in Europe. Many times the only bread available was whole grain dark bread. Often the bread was very heavy because a lot of bran was used to stretch the flour supply. After the war, this light bread, which has a fairly soft crust because it is made with milk, became popular. It makes good sandwiches.

1 cake yeast
2 cups warm (110° F.) milk
1 teaspoon vegetable oil
1 teaspoon sorghum or sugar
1 teaspoon salt
Approximately 5 1/2 to 6 cups unbleached
   all-purpose flour

Yield: 2 medium-size loaves

In a 6-quart mixing bowl, dissolve the yeast in the milk. Add the remaining ingredients, mixing the salt in with the flour, and work them into the dough.

Turn the dough out onto a lightly floured surface and knead it for 6 to 7 minutes.

Return the dough to the mixing bowl and cover it with a towel. Let the dough rise in a warm (75° F.) place for 1 hour, or until doubled in bulk.

Divide the dough into 2 equal halves and shape each piece into an oblong loaf. Set the loaves on a baking sheet that has been lightly greased with vegetable shortening. Cover the loaves with a towel and let them rise again for 50 minutes.

Bake in a preheated 400° F. oven for 35 minutes, or until golden brown. Remove from the baking sheet at once and cool on a wire rack.

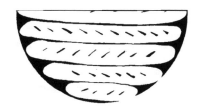

Limburger Miner's Bread

This is a very old recipe from the province of Limburg in Holland. This bread has nothing in common with the strong Limburger cheese. But it is a favorite in that province, and it is eaten by the hard-working coal miners around the city of Maastricht. This bread has a fine texture and flavor. Serve it warm.

1 cake yeast
2 cups warm (110° F.) skim milk
Approximately 6 1/4 cups unbleached
  all-purpose flour
1 tablespoon vegetable oil
1 tablespoon honey
3 eggs, at room temperature, lightly beaten
Pinch mace (optional)
1 teaspoon salt

Yield: 2 medium-size round loaves

In a 6-quart mixing bowl, dissolve the yeast in 1 cup of the skim milk. Add 1 cup of the flour. Mix well. Let this ferment for 3 1/2 hours in a warm (75° F.) place. Then add the rest of the yeast and the milk. Mix well. Add the remaining ingredients, and work into a dough.

Turn the dough out onto a lightly floured surface and knead it for 6 to 7 minutes.

Return the dough to the mixing bowl and cover it with a towel. Let the dough rise in a warm (75° F.) place for 1 hour, or until doubled in bulk.

Divide the dough into 2 equal halves and shape each piece into a round loaf. Set the loaves on a lightly greased baking sheet. Cover with a towel and let rise again for 50 minutes.

Bake in a preheated 350° F. oven for 45 to 50 minutes. Remove the loaves from the baking sheet at once and cool on a wire rack.

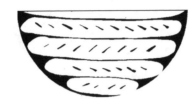

Scandinavian Potato Bread

Velkommen *(welcome) to the land of the Vikings. This old Scandinavian recipe is truly remarkable. The soft loaves stay fresh for days. The cake-like bread tastes delicious, especially with herring in wine sauce or with smoked ham.*

1 cake yeast
2 cups warm (110° F.) potato cooking water
1 medium-size potato, boiled and mashed
Approximately 6 cups unbleached
  all-purpose flour
1 teaspoon vegetable oil
4 teaspoons honey or sugar
1 egg, at room temperature, lightly beaten
1 teaspoon salt

Yield: 2 medium-sized round loaves

In a 6-quart mixing bowl, dissolve the yeast in the water. Add the potato and 1 cup of the flour. Mix well. Let this ferment for 1 hour in a warm (75° F.) place. Then add the remaining ingredients, mixing the salt with the remaining 5 cups flour, and work them into a dough.

Turn the dough out on a lightly floured surface and knead it for 6 to 7 minutes.

Return the dough to the mixing bowl and cover it with a towel. Let the dough rise in a warm (75° F.) place for 1 hour, or until doubled in bulk.

Divide the dough into 2 equal halves and shape each piece into a round loaf. Set the loaves on a baking sheet that has been liberally dusted with cornmeal. Cover the loaves and let them rise again for 50 minutes.

Bake in a preheated 375° F. oven for 40 minutes. Remove the loaves from the baking sheet at once and cool on a wire rack.

Crusty Garlic Bread

This subtly flavored Old World sourdough makes an excellent accompaniment to soup or pasta. It won first place in 1974 at the Wyoming State Fair. Garlic lovers will want to increase the amount of garlic.

1 cake yeast
2 cups warm (110° F.) water
Approximately 6 cups unbleached all-purpose
   flour
1 teaspoon corn or vegetable oil
1 egg white, at room temperature
1 small clove fresh garlic, crushed
1/2 teaspoon garlic powder
1 teaspoon salt

Yield: 3 small loaves

In a 6-quart mixing bowl, dissolve half of the yeast in 1 cup of the water. Add 1 cup of the flour. Mix well. Let this ferment overnight in a warm (75° F.) place. Then add the rest of the yeast and the water. Mix well. Add the oil, sorghum, garlic, garlic powder, salt, and the remaining flour, and work them into a dough.

Turn the dough out onto a lightly floured surface and knead it for 6 to 7 minutes.

Return to the mixing bowl and cover it with a towel. Let rise in a warm (75° F.) place for 1 hour or until doubled in bulk.

Divide the dough into 3 equal parts and shape each into a long loaf. Set on a baking sheet that has been liberally dusted with cornmeal. Cover with a towel and let rise again for 50 minutes.

Bake in a preheated 400° F. oven for 30 minutes. Remove the loaves from the baking sheet at once and cool on a wire rack.

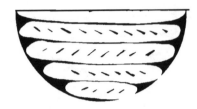

Herb Bread

A recipe from the European breadbasket—the Ukraine. There you will find a greater variety of bread than anywhere else in Europe. As a sign of hospitality, even in these modern times, it is customary among Ukrainians to break bread with visitors and share it with salt.

1 cake yeast
2 cups warm (110° F.) water
2 teaspoons vegetable oil
1 teaspoon honey or sugar
2 eggs, at room temperature, lightly beaten
1 teaspoon finely chopped fresh parsley
1/2 teaspoon caraway seeds
1/4 teaspoon cumin seeds
Pinch nutmeg
1 teaspoon salt
Approximately 6 cups unbleached all-purpose
    flour

Yield: 2 medium-size loaves

In a 6-quart mixing bowl, dissolve the yeast in the water. Add the remaining ingredients, mixing the salt in with the flour, and work them into a dough.

Turn the dough out onto a lightly floured surface and knead it for 6 to 7 minutes.

Return the dough to the mixing bowl and cover with a towel. Let rise in a warm (75° F.) place for 1 hour, or until doubled in bulk.

Divide the dough into 2 equal halves and shape each into an oblong loaf. Set the loaves on a lightly greased baking sheet. Cover with a towel and let them rise again for 50 minutes.

Bake in a preheated 375° F. oven for 50 minutes, or until golden brown. Remove from the baking sheet at once and cool on a wire rack.

This bread should cool for at least 1 hour before it is served.

Dill Bread

This very popular Old World recipe makes a real family-pleasing bread. The dill gives a buttery flavor to the bread, and the texture is quite soft due to the cottage cheese.

1 cake yeast
1 1/2 cups warm (110° F.) water
2 teaspoons honey or sugar
2 eggs, at room temperature, lightly beaten
1 cup cottage cheese, at room temperature
2 teaspoons dill seeds
1 teaspoon salt
Approximately 5 1/2 to 6 cups unbleached all-purpose flour

Yield: 2 medium-size loaves

In a 6-quart mixing bowl, dissolve the yeast in the water. Add the remaining ingredients, mixing the salt in with the flour, and work them into a dough.

Turn the dough out onto a lightly floured surface and knead it for 6 to 7 minutes, until the dough is smooth, elastic, and somewhat glossy.

Return the dough to the mixing bowl and cover it with a towel. Let the dough rise in a warm (75° F.) place for 1 hour, or until doubled in bulk.

Divide the dough into 2 equal halves and shape each piece into an oblong loaf. Set the loaves on a baking sheet that has been lightly greased with vegetable shortening. Cover the loaves with a towel and let them rise again for 55 minutes.

Bake in a preheated 375° F. oven for 50 minutes, or until golden brown. Remove the loaves from the baking sheet at once and allow them to cool on a wire rack.

Wheat Germ Bread

The added wheat germ gives this bread a pleasant nut-like flavor. This Dutch recipe was entered in the Wyoming State Fair in 1972 and won first prize.

1 cake yeast
2 cups warm (110° F.) water
2 teaspoons vegetable oil
2 teaspoons honey or sugar
1 egg, at room temperature, lightly beaten
1/2 cup wheat germ
1 teaspoon salt
Approximately 5 1/2 cups unbleached
   all-purpose flour

Yield: 2 medium-size loaves

In a 6-quart mixing bowl, dissolve the yeast in the water. Add the remaining ingredients, mixing the salt in with the flour, and work them into a dough.

Turn the dough out onto a lightly floured surface and knead it for 6 to 7 minutes, until the dough is smooth, elastic, and glossy.

Return the dough to the mixing bowl and cover it with a towel. Let the dough rise in a warm (75° F.) place for 45 to 50 minutes, or until doubled in bulk.

Divide the dough into 2 equal halves and shape each piece into an oblong loaf. Set the loaves on a baking sheet that has been lightly greased with vegetable shortening. Cover the loaves with a towel and let them rise again for 45 minutes.

Bake in a preheated 375° F. oven for 45 minutes. Remove the loaves from the baking sheet at once and cool on a wire rack.

Scotch-Style Oat Bread

You don't have to be a bagpiper and wear a kilt to really enjoy this Scotch-style oat bread. This is a light tasty bread that is delicious toasted and served with strawberry jam for breakfast.

1 cake yeast
1 cup warm (110° F.) water
1 cup uncooked rolled oats
1 cup warm (110° F.) milk
2 teaspoons vegetable oil
2 teaspoons sorghum or sugar
1 egg, at room temperature, lightly beaten
1 teaspoon salt
Approximately 5 cups unbleached all-purpose
  flour

Yield: 2 medium-size loaves

In a 6-quart mixing bowl, dissolve the yeast in the water. Add the oats. Mix well. Let stand for 20 minutes. Then add the milk and the remaining ingredients, mixing the salt with the flour, and work them into a dough.

Turn the dough out onto a lightly floured surface and knead it for 6 to 7 minutes.

Return the dough to the mixing bowl and cover with a towel. Let rise in a warm (75° F.) place for 1 hour, or until doubled in bulk.

Divide the dough into 2 equal halves and shape each piece into an oblong loaf. Set the loaves on a baking sheet that has been lightly greased with vegetable shortening and sprinkled with 2 or 3 teaspoons rolled oats. Cover the loaves with a towel and let them rise again for 45 to 50 minutes.

Bake in a preheated 375° F. oven for 40 minutes. Remove the loaves from the baking sheet at once and cool on a wire rack.

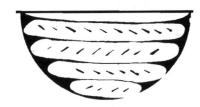

Dutch-Style Sourdough White Bread

Don't expect the strong flavor of a San Francisco-style sourdough from this recipe. Often San Francisco sourdoughs are soured with vinegar, whereas this bread is naturally soured. It is a favorite from my childhood, made without the addition of sweeteners or shortening. This bread should be eaten fresh. It is crusty on the outside, soft on the inside, and has a delicious yeasty flavor.

1 1/4 cakes yeast (or 4 teaspoons dry yeast)
2 cups warm (110° F.) water
Approximately 6 cups unbleached
  all-purpose flour
1 teaspoon salt

Yield: 2 medium-size round loaves

In a 1-quart glass jar, mix 1/2 cup of the water with 1/2 cup of the flour and 1/4 cake yeast (or 1 teaspoon dry yeast). Allow this mixture to ferment overnight (for 12 hours) in the uncovered jar in a warm (75° F.) place. Then pour this sour mixture into a 6-quart mixing bowl and add the remaining 1 cake yeast (or 3 teaspoons dry yeast) and the 1 1/2 cups water. Mix well. Add the salt mixed with the remaining 5 1/2 cups of flour and work into a dough.

Turn the dough out onto a lightly floured surface and knead it for 6 to 7 minutes, until the dough is smooth, elastic, and somewhat glossy.

Return the dough to the mixing bowl and cover it with a towel. Let the dough rise in a warm (75° F.) place for 1 hour or until doubled in bulk.

Divide the dough into 2 equal halves and shape each piece into a round loaf. Set the loaves on a baking sheet that has been liberally dusted with cornmeal. Cover the loaves with a towel and let them rise again for 45 minutes.

Bake in a preheated 400° F. oven for 40 minutes, or until golden brown. Remove the loaves from the baking sheet at once and allow them to cool on a wire rack.

Soy Bread

During World War II, wheat was in short supply, and so bakers used whatever was available and sometimes it was soy. Soy flour does have a distinctive bean flavor. I think it makes for a tasty bread, very good for sandwiches.

1 cake yeast
2 cups warm (110° F.) water
1 teaspoon vegetable oil
2 teaspoons honey or sugar
2 eggs, at room temperature, lightly beaten
1 teaspoon salt
1 cup soy flour
Approximately 5 cups unbleached all-purpose
  flour

Yield: 2 medium-size loaves

In a 6-quart mixing bowl, dissolve the yeast in the water. Add the remaining ingredients, mixing the salt with the flour, and work them into a dough.

Turn the dough out onto a lightly floured surface and knead it for 6 to 7 minutes, until the dough is smooth, elastic, and glossy.

Return the dough to the mixing bowl and cover it with a towel. Let the dough rise in a warm (75° F.) place for 50 minutes, or until doubled in bulk.

Divide the dough into 2 equal halves and shape each into an oblong loaf. Set on a baking sheet that has been lightly greased with vegetable shortening. Cover with a towel and let them rise again, for 45 minutes.

Bake in a preheated 375° F. oven for 45 minutes, or until golden brown. Remove the loaves from the baking sheet at once and allow them to cool on a wire rack.

3
Whole Grain Breads

Dark Wheat Bread

This basic whole grain recipe was a winner at both the 1975 Platte County Fair and the 1975 Wyoming State Fair. It has a pleasant whole grain flavor and is delicious when served fresh with butter and cheese.

1 cake yeast
2 cups warm (110° F.) water
1 teaspoon vegetable oil
1 teaspoon honey
1 teaspoon salt
2 cups unbleached all-purpose flour
Approximately 4 cups whole wheat flour

Yield: 2 medium-size loaves

In a 6-quart mixing bowl, dissolve the yeast in the water. Add the remaining ingredients, mixing the salt in with the flour, and work them into a dough.

Turn the dough out onto a lightly floured surface and knead it for 6 to 7 minutes, until the dough is smooth, elastic, and glossy.

Return the dough to the mixing bowl and cover it with a towel. Let the dough rise in a warm (75° F.) place for 45 minutes, or until doubled in bulk.

Divide the dough into 2 equal halves and shape each piece into an oblong loaf. Set the loaves on a baking sheet that has been lightly greased with vegetable shortening. Cover with a towel and let rise again for 45 minutes.

Bake in a preheated 375° F. oven for 45 minutes, or until golden brown. Remove the loaves from the baking sheet at once and allow them to cool on a wire rack.

Farmer's Wheat Bread

Known as Dutch Boeren Tarve Brood, *this bread originated in the farms around Axel, a small city in the Dutch part of Flanders, where the farmers' wives baked bread only once a week, usually on Fridays. This slightly sweet, moist bread will keep for a week in a bread box. It makes good sandwiches and tasty French toast.*

1 cake yeast
1 cup warm (110° F.) water
1 cup warm (110° F.) milk
1 teaspoon vegetable oil
2 teaspoons honey or sugar
1 egg, at room temperature, slightly beaten
1 teaspoon salt
3 cups whole wheat flour
Approximately 3 cups unbleached
   all-purpose flour

Yield: 2 medium-size loaves

In a 6-quart mixing bowl, dissolve the yeast in the water. Add the milk. Mix well. Add the remaining ingredients, mixing the salt with the flours, and work them into a dough.

Turn the dough out onto a lightly floured surface and knead it for 6 to 7 minutes, until the dough is smooth, elastic, and glossy.

Return the dough to the mixing bowl and cover it with a towel. Let the dough rise in a warm (75° F.) place for 50 minutes, or until doubled in bulk.

Divide the dough into 2 equal halves and shape each piece into an oblong loaf. Set the loaves on a baking sheet that has been lightly greased with vegetable shortening. Cover the loaves with a towel and let them rise again for 50 minutes.

Bake in a preheated 375° F. oven for 40 minutes, or until golden brown. Remove the loaves from the baking sheet at once and allow them to cool on a wire rack.

Whole Wheat Buttermilk Bread

Buttermilk gives bread a slightly tangy flavor, and breads made with buttermilk usually rise higher than breads made with milk or water. This Dutch recipe makes a beautiful light wheat bread that is wonderful served warm with butter and cheese.

1 cake yeast
2 cups warm (110° F.) buttermilk
1 teaspoon vegetable oil
2 teaspoons sorghum or sugar
1 teaspoon salt
3 cups whole wheat flour
Approximately 3 cups unbleached all-purpose flour

Yield: 2 medium-size loaves

In a 6-quart mixing bowl, dissolve the yeast in the buttermilk. Add the remaining ingredients, mixing the salt with the flours, and work them into a dough.

Turn the dough out onto a lightly floured surface and knead it for 6 to 7 minutes, until the dough is smooth, elastic, and somewhat glossy.

Return the dough to the mixing bowl and cover it with a towel. Let the dough rise in a warm (75° F.) place for 45 minutes, or until doubled in bulk.

Divide the dough into 2 equal halves and shape each piece into an oblong loaf. Set the loaves on a baking sheet that has been liberally dusted with cornmeal. Cover the loaves with a towel and let them rise again for 45 minutes.

Bake in a preheated 375° F. oven for 45 minutes, or until golden brown. Remove the loaves from the baking sheet at once and allow them to cool on a wire rack.

Light Buttermilk Wheat Bread

Bounded by the Rhine and Thur rivers and by the lake of Zurich is the fertile area of the canton of Zurich, in Switzerland. The lake itself is noted for its idyllic scenery, and the whole region is very picturesque. From there came the recipe for this light wheat bread. Try it – it might make you yodel.

1 cake yeast
2 cups warm (110° F.) buttermilk
1 teaspoon salt
4 cups unbleached all-purpose flour
Approximately 2 cups whole wheat flour

Yield: 2 medium-size loaves

In a 6-quart mixing bowl, dissolve the yeast in the buttermilk. Add the remaining ingredients, mixing the salt with the flours, and work them into a dough.

Turn the dough out onto a lightly floured surface and knead it for 6 to 7 minutes, until the dough is smooth, elastic, and somewhat glossy. Return the dough to the mixing bowl and cover it with a towel. Let the dough rise in a warm (75° F.) place for 50 minutes, or until doubled in bulk.

Divide the dough into 2 equal halves and shape each piece into an oblong loaf. Set the loaves on a baking sheet that has been lightly greased with vegetable shortening. Cover the loaves with a towel and let them rise again for 45 minutes.

Bake in a preheated 375° F. oven for 45 minutes, or until golden brown. Remove the loaves from the baking sheet at once and allow them to cool on a wire rack.

Old-Fashioned Wheat Bread

This is an old recipe from the Dutch island of Vlieland. It makes a nice natural brown bread that tastes somewhat like rye because of the subtle caraway flavor. This bread is part of the regular diet of the fishermen who live on this island. It is delicious with kippered herring and Dutch beer.

1 cake yeast
2 cups warm (110° F.) milk
2 teaspoons vegetable oil
1 tablespoon sorghum or sugar
1/2 teaspoon caraway seeds, finely ground
1 teaspoon salt
Approximately 5 1/2 cups whole wheat flour

Yield: 2 small round loaves

In a 6-quart mixing bowl, dissolve the yeast in the milk. Add the remaining ingredients, mixing the salt with the flour, and work them into a dough.

Turn the dough out onto a lightly floured surface and knead it for 6 to 7 minutes, until the dough is smooth, elastic, and somewhat glossy.

Return the dough to the mixing bowl and cover it with a towel. Let the dough rise in a warm (75° F.) place for 50 minutes, or until doubled in bulk.

Divide the dough into 2 equal halves and shape each piece into a round loaf. Set the loaves on a baking sheet that has been liberally dusted with cornmeal. Cover the loaves with a towel and let them rise again for 50 minutes.

Bake in a preheated 375° F. oven for 45 minutes. Remove the loaves from the baking sheet at once and allow them to cool on a wire rack.

Ella's 100% Wheat Bread

My wife's family emigrated to Brazil from Germany in 1910. They always baked their bread at home in Germany. In Brazil, they did so in a mud and brick oven. When they moved to the big city of São Paulo later on, they used a gas oven. In one of my visits there I built a mud and brick oven, and it made a big difference in the taste of the bread. You can experience the same difference in your own home by following the instructions for creating a brick oven effect with a clay pot saucer on page 15. This recipe, which makes a heavy bread, is in memory of my mother-in-law.

1 cake yeast
2 cups warm (110° F.) potato cooking water
1 teaspoon salt
Approximately 5 1/2 cups whole wheat flour

Yield: 2 medium-size loaves

In a 6-quart mixing bowl, dissolve the yeast in the potato cooking water. Add the remaining ingredients, mixing the salt with the flour, and work them into a dough.

Turn the dough out onto a lightly floured surface and knead it for 6 to 7 minutes, until the dough is smooth, elastic, and glossy.

Return the dough to the mixing bowl and cover it with a towel. Let the dough rise in a warm (75° F.) place for 50 minutes, or until doubled in bulk.

Divide the dough into 2 equal halves and shape each piece into an oblong loaf. Set the loaves on a baking sheet that has been lightly greased with vegetable shortening. Cover the loaves with a towel and let them rise again for 45 minutes.

Bake in a preheated 400° F. oven for 35 minutes, or until golden brown. Remove the loaves from the baking sheet at once and allow them to cool on a wire rack.

Workman's Bread

This beautiful dark brown bread was baked only once a week, on Fridays, in my grandfather's bakery. Since it contained a lot of bran, it could be sold for 3 cents less than other breads. Many of the poor working people used to buy this bread and so it came to be called Workman's Bread. Today, many people are looking for ways to add bran, a good source of fiber, to their diets. This grainy bread is guaranteed to be satisfying.

1 cake yeast
2 cups warm (110° F.) water
2 teaspoons vegetable oil
1 cup bran
1 teaspoon salt
2 cups whole wheat flour
Approximately 2 1/2 to 3 cups unbleached
   all-purpose flour

Yield: 2 small round loaves

In a 6-quart mixing bowl, dissolve the yeast in the water. Add the remaining ingredients, mixing the salt with the flours, and work them into a dough.

Turn the dough out onto a lightly floured surface and knead it for 6 to 7 minutes, until the dough is smooth, elastic, and glossy.

Return the dough to the mixing bowl and cover it with a towel. Let the dough rise in a warm (75° F.) place for 50 minutes, or until doubled in bulk.

Divide the dough into 2 equal halves and shape each piece into a round loaf. Set the loaves on a baking sheet that has been liberally dusted with cornmeal. Cover the loaves with a towel and let them rise again for 45 to 50 minutes.

Bake in a preheated 400° F. oven for 35 minutes. Remove the loaves from the baking sheet at once and allow them to cool on a wire rack.

Honey Bran Bread

This recipe originated in Antwerp, where the bakers were also vendors of their own products. These bakers would push carts stacked high with 5 or 6 kinds of bread. Ringing a large copper bell, they would shout at the top of their voices praising and recommending their baked goods while running down their competitors' breads.

1 cake yeast
2 cups warm (110° F.) water
2 teaspoons vegetable oil
4 teaspoons honey
2 eggs, at room temperature, lightly beaten
1 cup bran
1 teaspoon salt
Approximately 5 cups unbleached all-purpose
    flour

Yield: 2 medium-size round loaves

In a 6-quart mixing bowl, dissolve the yeast in the water. Add all the remaining ingredients, mixing the salt with the flour, and work them into a dough.

Turn the dough out onto a lightly floured surface and knead it for 6 to 7 minutes, until the dough is smooth, elastic, and glossy.

Return the dough to the mixing bowl and cover it with a towel. Let the dough rise in a warm (75° F.) place for 50 minutes, or until doubled in bulk.

Divide the dough into 2 equal halves and shape each piece into a round loaf. Set the loaves on a baking sheet that has been liberally dusted with cornmeal. Cover the loaves with a towel and let them rise again for 50 minutes.

Bake in a preheated 375° F. oven for 40 minutes, or until golden brown. Remove the loaves from the baking sheet at once and allow them to cool on a wire rack.

Golden Graham Bread

This traditional English bread is often used to make fried bread. The bread is thickly sliced, then fried in the same pan in which bacon was fried. It is usually served for breakfast with bacon, eggs, and marmalade. And, of course, a good cup of tea.

1 cake yeast
2 cups warm (110° F.) milk
2 teaspoons vegetable oil
1 teaspoon honey or sugar
2 eggs, at room temperature, lightly beaten
1 teaspoon salt
3 cups graham flour
Approximately 3 cups unbleached all-purpose flour

Yield: 2 medium-size loaves

In a 6-quart mixing bowl, dissolve the yeast in the milk. Add the remaining ingredients, mixing the salt with the flours, and work them into a dough.

Turn the dough out onto a lightly floured surface and knead it for 6 to 7 minutes, until the dough is smooth, elastic, and glossy.

Return the dough to the mixing bowl and cover it with a towel. Let the dough rise in a warm (75° F.) place for 50 minutes, or until doubled in bulk.

Divide the dough into 2 equal halves and shape each piece into an oblong loaf. Set the loaves on a baking sheet that has been lightly greased with vegetable shortening. Cover the loaves with a towel and let them rise again for 45 minutes.

Bake in a preheated 375° F. oven for 45 minutes, or until golden brown. Remove the loaves from the baking sheet at once and allow them to cool on a wire rack.

Graham Bread

∞∞

In Austria people like to take their time to eat. They sit around sipping wine and enjoy their bread along with cheese and some cold meats. They eat slowly, because the most important and satisfying accompaniment is lots of conversation.

This recipe makes a bread that is crustier and has a more pronounced whole grain flavor than the previous recipes.

1 cake yeast
2 cups warm (110° F.) water
2 teaspoons vegetable oil
1 teaspoon salt
2 cups graham flour
Approximately 4 cups unbleached all-purpose flour

Yield: 2 medium-size round loaves

In a 6-quart mixing bowl, dissolve the yeast in the water. Add the remaining ingredients, mixing the salt with the flours, and work them into a dough.

Turn the dough out onto a lightly floured surface and knead it 6 to 7 minutes, until the dough is smooth, elastic, and somewhat glossy.

Return the dough to the mixing bowl and cover it with a towel. Let the dough rise in a warm (75° F.) place for 50 minutes, or until doubled in bulk.

Divide the dough into 2 equal halves and shape each piece into a round loaf. Set the loaves on a baking sheet that has been liberally dusted with cornmeal. Cover the loaves with a towel and let them rise again for 50 minutes.

Bake in a preheated 375° F. oven for 50 minutes, or until golden brown. Remove the loaves from the baking sheet at once and allow them to cool on a wire rack.

Wartime Millet Bread

This bread was baked during the second world war in some parts of Europe. Because wheat was then in short supply, bakers had to stretch their supply with whatever other grains they could get. In many places millet was often available. People liked the taste of this bread so even after the war, there was a demand for it. These days, in this country, millet flour is available in most health food stores.

1 cake yeast
2 cups warm (110° F.) water
1 1/2 cups millet flour
2 teaspoons vegetable oil
2 teaspoons honey or sugar
1 teaspoon salt
Approximately 4 1/2 cups whole wheat flour

Yield: 2 medium-size round loaves

In a 6-quart mixing bowl, dissolve the yeast in the water. Add the millet flour and mix well. Add the remaining ingredients, mixing the salt with the flour, and work them into a dough.

Turn the dough out onto a lightly floured surface and knead it for 6 to 7 minutes, until the dough is smooth, elastic, and glossy.

Return the dough to the mixing bowl and cover it with a towel. Let the dough rise in a warm (75° F.) place for 45 minutes, or until doubled in bulk.

Divide the dough into 2 equal halves and shape each piece into a round loaf. Set the loaves on a baking sheet that has been liberally dusted with cornmeal. Cover with a towel and let rise again for 45 minutes.

Bake in a preheated 375° F. oven for 50 minutes, or until golden brown. Remove the loaves from the baking sheet at once and allow them to cool on a wire rack.

Dutch Cracked Wheat Bread

This is a real crunchy, chewy bread for hardy bread eaters, a bread to enjoy with cold cuts, cheese, smoked meats, and plenty of Dutch beer.

1 cup cracked wheat (available at natural food stores)
2 cups warm (110° F.) water
1 cake yeast
1 teaspoon vegetable oil
2 teaspoons molasses
1 egg, at room temperature, lightly beaten
1 teaspoon salt
Approximately 5 cups unbleached all-purpose flour

Yield: 2 medium-size round loaves

In a 6-quart mixing bowl, soak the cracked wheat in the water for 1 hour. Then dissolve the yeast in this mixture. Add the remaining ingredients, mixing the salt with the flour, and work them into a dough.

Turn the dough out onto a lightly floured surface and knead it for 6 to 7 minutes, until the dough is smooth, elastic, and glossy.

Return the dough to the mixing bowl and cover it with a towel. Let the dough rise in a warm (75° F.) place for 50 minutes, or until doubled in bulk.

Divide the dough into 2 equal halves and shape each piece into a round loaf. Set the loaves on a baking sheet that has been liberally dusted with cornmeal. Cover with a towel and let rise again for 50 minutes.

Bake in a preheated 375° F. oven for 45 minutes, or until golden brown. Remove the loaves from the baking sheet at once and allow them to cool on a wire rack.

Whole Wheat Oatmeal Bread

This grainy, robustly flavored, dark brown bread goes well with Irish stew. Serve it warm, with butter.

1 cake yeast
2 cups warm (110° F.) water
2 teaspoons vegetable oil
1 teaspoon honey or sugar
2 eggs, at room temperature, lightly beaten
1 cup uncooked rolled oats
1 teaspoon salt
4 cups whole wheat flour
Approximately 1 cup unbleached
   all-purpose flour

Yield: 2 small round loaves

In a 6-quart mixing bowl, dissolve the yeast in the water. Add the remaining ingredients, mixing the salt with the flours, and work them into a dough.

Turn the dough out onto a lightly floured surface and knead it for 6 to 7 minutes, until the dough is smooth, elastic, and glossy.

Return the dough to the mixing bowl and cover it with a towel. Let the dough rise in a warm (75° F.) place for 50 minutes, or until doubled in bulk.

Divide the dough into 2 equal halves and shape each piece into a round loaf. Set the loaves on a baking sheet that has been liberally dusted with cornmeal. Cover the loaves with a towel and let them rise again for 50 minutes.

Bake in a preheated 375° F. oven for 45 minutes, or until golden brown. Remove the loaves from the baking sheet at once and allow them to cool on a wire rack.

Barley Bread

You can buy barley flour at some supermarkets or at most natural food stores. You can also grind your own flour from barley if you have a good blender or an electric mill.

Barley flour gives bread a sweet flavor and a tacky texture. Even when the loaves are fully baked, they retain the slightly sticky feel one associates with underbaked bread.

1 cake yeast
2 cups warm (110° F.) water
1 teaspoon vegetable oil
1 tablespoon honey or sugar
1 egg, at room temperature, lightly beaten
1 teaspoon salt
1 1/2 cups barley flour
Approximately 4 1/2 cups unbleached
   all-purpose flour

Yield: 2 medium-size loaves

In a 6-quart mixing bowl, dissolve the yeast in the water. Add all the remaining ingredients, mixing the salt with the flours, and work them into a dough.

Turn the dough out onto a lightly floured surface and knead it for 6 to 7 minutes, until the dough is smooth, elastic, and glossy.

Return the dough to the mixing bowl and cover it with a towel. Let the dough rise in a warm (75° F.) place for 50 minutes, or until doubled in bulk.

Divide the dough into 2 equal halves and shape each piece into an oblong loaf. Set the loaves on a baking sheet that has been lightly greased with vegetable shortening. Cover the loaves with a towel and let them rise again for 50 minutes.

Bake in a preheated 375° F. oven for 45 minutes, or until golden brown. Remove the loaves from the baking sheet at once and allow them to cool on a wire rack.

Multi-Grain Bread

This hearty bread is moist and has a delicious nutty flavor. It makes very good sandwiches. Slice thinly and serve with kippered herring, onions, and pickles. And a stein of beer.

1 cake yeast
2 cups warm (110° F.) water
1 teaspoon vegetable oil
2 teaspoons honey or sugar
1 egg, at room temperature, lightly beaten
1/4 cup cornmeal
1/4 cup uncooked rolled oats
1 teaspoon salt
1/4 cup rye flour
1/4 cup soy flour
1/4 cup buckwheat flour
Approximately 4 3/4 cups unbleached
　all-purpose flour

Yield: 2 medium-size loaves

In a 6-quart mixing bowl, dissolve the yeast in the water. Add the remaining ingredients, mixing the salt with the flours, and work them into a dough.

Turn the dough out onto a lightly floured surface and knead it for 6 to 7 minutes, until the dough is smooth, elastic, and glossy.

Return the dough to the mixing bowl and cover it with a towel. Let the dough rise in a warm (75° F.) place for 50 minutes, or until doubled in bulk.

Divide the dough into 2 equal halves and shape each piece into an oblong loaf. Set the loaves on a baking sheet that has been lightly greased with vegetable shortening. Cover the loaves with a towel and let them rise again for 50 minutes.

Bake in a preheated 375° F. oven for 45 minutes, or until golden brown. Remove the loaves from the baking sheet at once and allow them to cool on a wire rack.

Buckwheat Bread

If you like buckwheat pancakes with their slightly bitter flavor, you'll like this bread. This old recipe came from the border region between Austria and Slovenia, in Yugoslavia. It is usually served with a thick potato soup that is spiced with caraway seeds—a perfect combination.

1 cake yeast
2 cups warm (110° F.) water
1 teaspoon vegetable oil
2 teaspoons honey or sugar
1 egg, at room temperature, lightly beaten
1 teaspoon salt
1/2 cup buckwheat flour
Approximately 5 3/4 cups unbleached
   all-purpose flour

Yield: 2 medium-size loaves

In a 6-quart mixing bowl, dissolve the yeast in the water. Add the remaining ingredients, mixing the salt with the flours, and work them into a dough.

Turn the dough out onto a lightly floured surface and knead it for 6 to 7 minutes, until the dough is smooth, elastic, and glossy.

Return the dough to the mixing bowl and cover it with a towel. Let the dough rise in a warm (75° F.) place for 50 minutes, or until doubled in bulk.

Divide the dough into 2 equal halves and shape each piece into an oblong loaf. Set the loaves on a baking sheet that has been lightly greased with vegetable shortening. Cover the loaves with a towel and let them rise again for 50 minutes.

Bake in a preheated 375° F. oven for 45 minutes, or until golden brown. Remove the loaves from the baking sheet at once and allow them to cool on a wire rack.

Swiss Shepherd's Bread

The Swiss are hard-working people who enjoy good food and wine. It's a joy to wake up in a hotel in Switzerland and have a breakfast tray brought up with all kinds of different breads beautifully arranged in a basket—better yet if you have a view of the Alps with it. This bread will help you dream of Switzerland; you can add to the atmosphere by having fondue with it.

1 cake yeast
2 cups warm (110° F.) water
1 cup whole wheat flour
1 teaspoon vegetable oil
1 teaspoon sorghum or sugar
1 egg, at room temperature, lightly beaten
1 teaspoon salt
Approximately 5 cups unbleached all-purpose
    flour

Yield: 3 small round loaves

In a 6-quart mixing bowl, dissolve half the yeast in 1 cup of the water. Add 1 cup whole wheat flour. Mix well. Set aside to ferment for 3 1/2 hours in a warm (75° F.) place. After 3 1/2 hours, add the rest of the yeast and the remaining 1 cup warm water. Mix well. Add the remaining ingredients, mixing the salt with the flour, and work into a dough.

Turn the dough out onto a lightly floured surface and knead it for 6 to 7 minutes.

Return the dough to the mixing bowl and cover with a towel. Let rise in a warm (75° F.) place for 1 hour, or until doubled in bulk.

Divide the dough into 3 equal pieces and shape each into a round loaf. Set the loaves on a baking sheet that has been liberally dusted with cornmeal. Cover with a towel and let rise again for 50 minutes.

Bake in a preheated 375° F. oven for 45 minutes, or until golden brown. Remove the loaves from the baking sheet at once and allow them to cool on a wire rack.

4
Rye Breads

Plain Rye Bread

This German recipe is quite simple, yet it produces a delightful rye bread. It is very good for sandwiches made with cold cuts and mayonnaise and served with dill pickles.

1 cake yeast
2 cups warm (110° F.) water
2 teaspoons caraway seeds
1 teaspoon salt
1 cup light rye flour
Approximately 5 cups unbleached
   all-purpose flour

Yield: 2 medium-size round loaves

In a 6-quart mixing bowl, dissolve the yeast in the water. Add the remaining ingredients, mixing the salt with the flours, and work them into a dough.

Turn the dough out onto a lightly floured surface and knead it for 6 to 7 minutes, until the dough is smooth, elastic, and glossy.

Return the dough to the mixing bowl and cover it with a towel. Let the dough rise in a warm (75° F.) place for 1 hour, or until doubled in bulk.

Divide the dough into 2 equal halves and shape each piece into a round loaf. Set the loaves on a baking sheet that has been liberally dusted with cornmeal. Cover the loaves with a towel and let them rise again for 50 minutes.

Bake in a preheated 400° F. oven for 40 minutes, or until golden brown. Remove the loaves from the baking sheet at once and allow them to cool on a wire rack.

Wartime Dark Bread

This bread originated during World War II in Holland where the bakers used rye to stretch the wheat supply. This bread is very good when served warm, with butter. The potato will keep it moist for days.

1 cake yeast
2 cups warm (110° F.) water
1 teaspoon molasses
1 small raw potato, peeled and grated
1/2 cup cornmeal
1 teaspoon salt
1 cup light rye flour
Approximately 4 1/2 cups unbleached
 all-purpose flour

Yield: 2 medium-size round loaves

In a 6-quart mixing bowl, dissolve the yeast in the water. Add the remaining ingredients, mixing the salt with the flours, and work them into a dough.

Turn the dough out onto a lightly floured surface and knead it for only 4 minutes. Be careful not to overknead.

Return the dough to the mixing bowl and cover it with a towel. Let the dough rise in a warm place (75° F.) for 30 minutes.

Divide the dough into 2 equal halves and shape each piece into a round loaf. Set the loaves on a baking sheet that has been liberally dusted with cornmeal. Cover the loaves with a towel and let them rise again for 30 minutes.

Bake in a preheated 350° F. oven for 20 minutes. Then increase the oven temperature to 400° F. and bake for another 20 minutes. Remove the loaves from the baking sheet at once and allow them to cool on a wire rack.

Roughneck Bread

Dutch Rouwe-nek Brood *is a rib-sticking compact loaf that is a favorite with the dike builders in The Netherlands. These builders, who work long hours facing the northwestern winds that blow off the North Sea, are known by the general populace as "roughnecks."*

This bread is especially good after it has cooled and is sliced thin with a sharp knife. Serve it with a real Dutch cheese, such as Edam or Gouda, and wine, or with beer and kippered herring.

1 cake yeast
2 cups warm (110° F.) water
1 teaspoon molasses
1/2 cup bran
1 teaspoon salt
1 cup dark rye flour
Approximately 4 1/2 cups unbleached
   all-purpose flour

Yield: 2 small round loaves

In a 6-quart mixing bowl, dissolve the yeast in the water. Add the remaining ingredients, mixing the salt with the flours, and work them into a dough.

Turn the dough out onto a lightly floured surface and knead it for 6 to 7 minutes, until the dough is smooth, elastic, and glossy.

Return the dough to the mixing bowl and cover it with a towel. Let the dough rise in a warm (75° F.) place for 50 minutes, or until doubled in bulk.

Divide the dough into 2 equal halves and shape each piece into a round loaf. Set the loaves on a baking sheet that has been liberally dusted with cornmeal. Cover the loaves with a towel and let them rise again for 45 minutes.

Bake in a preheated 400° F. oven for 40 minutes, or until golden brown. Remove the loaves from the baking sheet at once and allow them to cool on a wire rack.

Black Forest Rye

This German recipe makes a coarse-grained loaf that has a natural dark color. It is traditionally eaten with Black Forest ham, which you sometimes can find in German delicatessens.

1 cake yeast
2 cups warm (110° F.) water
1 teaspoon vegetable oil
1 teaspoon molasses
1 teaspoon caraway seeds
1 teaspoon salt
2 cups dark rye flour
2 cups whole wheat flour
Approximately 2 cups unbleached all-purpose
  flour

Yield: 2 medium-size round loaves

In a 6-quart mixing bowl, dissolve the yeast in the water. Add the remaining ingredients, mixing the salt with the flours, and work them into a dough.

Turn the dough out onto a lightly floured surface and knead it for 6 to 7 minutes, until the dough is smooth, elastic, and glossy.

Return the dough to the mixing bowl and cover it with a towel. Let the dough rise in a warm (75° F.) place for 50 minutes, or until doubled in bulk.

Divide the dough into 2 equal halves and shape each piece into a round loaf. Set the loaves on a baking sheet that has been liberally dusted with cornmeal. Cover the loaves with a towel and let them rise again for 50 minutes.

Bake in a preheated 400° F. oven for 40 minutes, or until golden brown. Remove the loaves from the baking sheet at once and allow them to cool on a wire rack.

Original Black Bread

This is a very old German recipe for a compact loaf that is very satisfying and nutritious. It seems that the farther east you travel, the heavier the bread you will encounter. This bread is traditionally served with liverwurst or smoked or pickled meats, accompanied with hot potato salad and a good German brew.

1 cake yeast
2 cups warm (110° F.) water
1 teaspoon vegetable oil
2 teaspoons molasses
1 teaspoon caraway seeds
1 teaspoon salt
2 1/4 cups dark rye flour
Approximately 3 3/4 cups whole wheat flour

Yield: 2 medium-size loaves

In a 6-quart mixing bowl, dissolve the yeast in the water. Add the remaining ingredients, mixing the salt with the flours, and work them into a dough.

Turn the dough out onto a lightly floured surface and knead it for 6 to 7 minutes, until the dough is smooth, elastic, and glossy.

Return the dough to the mixing bowl and cover it with a towel. Let the dough rise in a warm place (75° F.) for 50 minutes, or until doubled in bulk.

Divide the dough into 2 equal halves and shape each piece into a round loaf. Set the loaves on a baking sheet that has been liberally dusted with cornmeal. Cover the loaves with a towel and let them rise again for 45 to 50 minutes.

Bake in a preheated 400° F. oven for 40 minutes, or until golden brown. Remove the loaves from the baking sheet at once and allow them to cool on a wire rack.

Old World Rye

There are breads for which Europe is unsurpassed. This Old World Rye is one of them. It is marvelously tasty, and it makes excellent Reuben sandwiches.

1 cake yeast
2 cups warm (110° F.) potato cooking water
1 teaspoon vegetable oil
2 teaspoons molasses
2 teaspoons caraway seeds
1 teaspoon salt
1 1/2 cups light rye flour
2 1/2 cups whole wheat flour
Approximately 2 cups unbleached all-purpose
   flour

Yield: 2 medium-size round loaves

In a 6-quart mixing bowl, dissolve the yeast in the water. Add the remaining ingredients, mixing the salt with the flours, and work them into a dough.

Turn the dough out onto a lightly floured surface and knead it for 6 to 7 minutes, until the dough is smooth, elastic, and glossy.

Return the dough to the mixing bowl and cover it with a towel. Let the dough rise in a warm (75° F.) place for 50 minutes, or until doubled in bulk.

Divide the dough into 2 equal halves and shape each piece into a round loaf. Set the loaves on a baking sheet that has been liberally dusted with cornmeal. Cover the loaves with a towel and let them rise again for 50 minutes.

Bake in a preheated 400° F. oven for 40 minutes, or until golden brown. Remove the loaves from the baking sheet at once and allow them to cool on a wire rack.

Dutch Country Bread

This recipe is very popular in Holland. Try it on a rainy day, with a good homemade soup. The rye flavor is very subtle.

1 cake yeast
2 cups warm (110° F.) water
1 cup light rye flour
2 teaspoons vegetable oil
2 teaspoons molasses
1 teaspoon salt
1 cup whole wheat flour
Approximately 4 cups unbleached all-purpose flour

Yield: 1 large round loaf

In a 6-quart mixing bowl, dissolve the yeast in the water. Add the rye flour. Mix well. Then add the remaining ingredients, mixing the salt with the flours, and work them into a dough.

Turn the dough out onto a lightly floured surface and knead it for 6 to 7 minutes, until the dough is smooth, elastic, and glossy.

Return the dough to the mixing bowl and cover it with a towel. Let the dough rise in a warm (75° F.) place for 45 minutes, or until doubled in bulk.

Shape the dough into 1 big round loaf. Set the loaf on a baking sheet that has been liberally dusted with cornmeal. Cover the loaf with a towel and let it rise again for 45 minutes.

Bake in a preheated 375° F. oven for 50 minutes, or until golden brown. Remove the loaf from the baking sheet at once and allow it to cool on a wire rack.

Old World Favorite

This delicious dark bread, which is grainy and light in texture, is a favorite with cheese and/or smoked meats and Dutch beer in the cafés around Amsterdam.

1 cake yeast
2 cups warm (110° F.) water
1 teaspoon vegetable oil
1 teaspoon molasses
1 egg, at room temperature, lightly beaten
2 teaspoons caraway seeds
1 teaspoon salt
1 cup dark rye flour
2 cups whole wheat flour
Approximately 3 cups unbleached all-purpose
   flour

Yield: 2 medium-size round loaves

In a 6-quart mixing bowl, dissolve the yeast in the water. Add the remaining ingredients, mixing the salt with the flours, and work them into a dough.

Turn the dough out onto a lightly floured surface and knead it for 6 to 7 minutes, until the dough is smooth, elastic, and glossy.

Return the dough to the mixing bowl and cover it with a towel. Let the dough rise in a warm (75° F.) place for 50 minutes, or until doubled in bulk.

Divide the dough into 2 equal halves and shape each piece into a round loaf. Set the loaves on a baking sheet that has been liberally dusted with cornmeal. Cover the loaves with a towel and let them rise again for 50 minutes.

Bake in a preheated 375° F. oven for 45 minutes, or until golden brown. Remove the loaves from the baking sheet at once and allow them to cool on a wire rack.

Northland Rye

Northern Germany is the region of dark rye breads and thick potato and cabbage soups, a good combination for wintry days. The potato cooking water keeps this bread fresh for days.

1 cake yeast
2 cups warm (110° F.) potato cooking water
1 cup dark rye flour
1 teaspoon vegetable oil
1 teaspoon sorghum or sugar
1 teaspoon caraway seeds
1 teaspoon salt
1 cup whole wheat flour
Approximately 4 cups unbleached all-purpose
    flour

Yield: 2 medium-size round loaves

In a 6-quart mixing bowl, dissolve half the yeast in 1 cup of the water. Add the rye flour. Mix well. Let this ferment for 3 1/2 hours in a warm (75° F.) place. Then add the rest of the yeast and water. Mix well. Add the remaining ingredients, mixing the salt with the flours, and work them into a dough.

Turn the dough out onto a lightly floured surface and knead it for 6 to 7 minutes, until the dough is smooth, elastic, and glossy.

Return the dough to the mixing bowl and cover with a towel. Let rise in a warm (75° F.) place for 1 hour, or until doubled in bulk.

Divide the dough into 2 equal halves and shape each into a round loaf. Set on a baking sheet that has been liberally dusted with cornmeal. Cover with a towel and let them rise again for 50 minutes.

Bake in a preheated 375° F. oven for 45 minutes, or until golden brown. Remove from the baking sheet at once and cool on a wire rack.

Bavarian Rye Bread

This is an excellent bread for Abendbrot, *the German evening meal. All that you need are some slices of this bread with mayonnaise or butter, some cold cuts or cheese, a little lettuce or some other greens, and you have a nutritious meal to top off your day.*

1 cake yeast
2 cups warm (110° F.) water
2 cups dark rye flour
1 teaspoon vegetable oil
1 teaspoon molasses
1 teaspoon caraway seeds
1 teaspoon salt
Approximately 3 1/2 to 4 cups unbleached
   all-purpose flour

Yield: 2 medium-size round loaves

In a 6-quart mixing bowl, dissolve half the yeast in 1 cup of the water. Add 1 cup of the dark rye flour. Mix well. Let this ferment for 3 1/2 hours in a warm (75° F.) place. Then add the rest of the yeast and the water. Mix well. Add the remaining ingredients, mixing the salt with the flours, and work them into a dough.

Turn the dough out onto a lightly floured surface and knead it for 6 to 7 minutes.

Return the dough to the mixing bowl and cover with a towel. Let rise in a warm (75° F.) place for 1 hour, or until doubled in bulk.

Divide the dough into 2 equal halves and shape each into a round loaf. Set on a baking sheet that has been liberally dusted with cornmeal. Cover the loaves with a towel and let them rise again for 50 minutes.

Bake in a preheated 400° F. oven for 40 minutes, or until golden brown. Remove from the baking sheet at once and cool on a wire rack.

Ella's Buttermilk Rye Bread

Ella, my mother-in-law, and her family emigrated from Europe to Brazil over 70 years ago. Along with other German immigrants, they literally hacked a town out of the woods, and they called it New Europe. In the hot, humid climate, and without refrigeration, milk turned sour quickly. Then it was used for bread baking. This buttermilk bread is very similar in flavor to the immigrants' bread. It rises well and has a pleasant tangy flavor.

1 cake yeast
2 cups warm (110° F.) buttermilk
1 cup dark rye flour
1 teaspoon vegetable oil
1 teaspoon caraway seeds
1 teaspoon salt
Approximately 5 cups unbleached all-purpose
   flour

Yield: 2 medium-size round loaves

In a 6-quart mixing bowl, dissolve the yeast in the buttermilk. Add the dark rye flour. Mix well. Let this ferment for 30 minutes in a warm (75° F.) place. Then add the remaining ingredients, mixing the salt with the remaining flour, and work them into a dough.

Turn the dough out onto a lightly floured surface and knead it for 6 to 7 minutes, until the dough is smooth, elastic, and glossy.

Return the dough to the mixing bowl and cover it with a towel. Let the dough rise in a warm (75° F.) place for 50 minutes, or until doubled in bulk.

Divide the dough into 2 equal halves and shape each piece into a round loaf. Set the loaves on a baking sheet that has been liberally dusted with cornmeal. Cover the loaves with a towel and let them rise again for 45 minutes.

Bake in a preheated 375° F. oven for 45 minutes, or until golden brown. Remove the loaves from the baking sheet at once and allow them to cool on a wire rack.

Dutch German Rye

∞∞

This delicious bread will stay fresh for days. In the Dutch German border region, this bread is traditionally served with sausage, a spicy mustard, and, of course, beer.

1 cake yeast
1 cup warm (110° F.) potato cooking water
2 cups dark rye flour
1 cup warm (110° F.) buttermilk
1 teaspoon vegetable oil
1 teaspoon molasses
1 small potato, peeled, boiled, and mashed
1 teaspoon caraway seeds
1 teaspoon salt
Approximately 4 cups unbleached all-purpose
  flour

Yield: 2 medium-size round loaves

In a 6-quart mixing bowl, dissolve the yeast in the potato cooking water. Add the rye flour. Mix well. Let this ferment for 30 minutes in a warm (75° F.) place. Then add the remaining ingredients, mixing the salt with the remaining flour, and work them into a dough.

Turn the dough out onto a lightly floured surface and knead it for 6 to 7 minutes, until the dough is smooth, elastic, and glossy.

Return the dough to the mixing bowl and cover it with a towel. Let the dough rise in a warm (75° F.) place for 50 minutes, or until doubled in bulk.

Divide the dough into 2 equal halves and shape each piece into a round loaf. Set the loaves on a baking sheet that has been liberally dusted with cornmeal. Cover the loaves with a towel and let them rise again for 50 minutes.

Bake in a preheated 375° F. oven for 45 minutes, or until golden brown. Remove the loaves from the baking sheet at once and allow them to cool on a wire rack.

Dark Buttermilk Rye

In the Ukraine the people prefer dark, heavy breads. This is a naturally dark bread that is delicious thickly sliced, spread with butter.

1 cake yeast
2 cups warm (110° F.) buttermilk
1 teaspoon caraway seeds
1 teaspoon salt
2 cups dark rye flour
2 cups whole wheat flour
Approximately 2 cups unbleached all-purpose flour

Yield: 2 medium-size round loaves

In a 6-quart mixing bowl, dissolve the yeast in the buttermilk. Add the remaining ingredients, mixing the salt with the flours, and work them into a dough.

Turn the dough out onto a lightly floured surface and knead it for 6 to 7 minutes, until the dough is smooth, elastic, and glossy.

Return the dough to the mixing bowl and cover it with a towel. Let the dough rise in a warm (75° F.) place for 50 minutes, or until doubled in bulk.

Divide the dough into 2 equal halves and shape each piece into a round loaf. Set the loaves on a baking sheet that has been liberally dusted with cornmeal. Cover the loaves with a towel and let them rise again for 50 minutes.

Bake in a preheated 400° F. oven for 35 to 40 minutes, or until golden brown. Remove the loaves from the baking sheet at once and allow them to cool on a wire rack.

Bulgarian Buttermilk Bread

This tangy, rich Bulgarian bread tastes like a delightful sourdough bread, but it does not require the time and work that goes with making a real sourdough. In Bulgaria they love to eat this bread with cheese and thinly sliced onions. Even without the onions, this is a delicious bread.

1 cake yeast
2 cups warm (110° F.) buttermilk
2 teaspoons vegetable oil
2 teaspoons sorghum or sugar
1 teaspoon sour cream
2 teaspoons caraway seeds
1 teaspoon salt
1 cup light rye flour
Approximately 5 cups unbleached all-purpose flour

Yield: 2 medium-size round loaves

In a 6-quart mixing bowl, dissolve the yeast in the buttermilk. Add the remaining ingredients, mixing the salt with the flours, and work them into a dough.

Turn the dough out onto a lightly floured surface and knead it for 6 to 7 minutes, until the dough is smooth, elastic, and glossy.

Return the dough to the mixing bowl and cover it with a towel. Let the dough rise in a warm (75° F.) place for 50 minutes, or until doubled in bulk.

Divide the dough into 2 equal halves and shape each piece into a round loaf. Set the loaves on a baking sheet that has been liberally dusted with cornmeal. Cover the loaves with a towel and let them rise again for 50 minutes.

Bake in a preheated 375° F. oven for 45 minutes, or until golden brown. Remove the loaves from the baking sheet at once and allow them to cool on a wire rack.

Kümmelbrot

The name translates as "cumin bread," and it's another very popular bread in Germany. It goes sehr gut *(very good)* with some bratwurst mit mustard and a stein of beer.

1 cake fresh yeast
2 cups warm (110° F.) water
1 teaspoon vegetable oil
1 teaspoon sorghum or sugar
1 teaspoon cumin seeds
1 teaspoon caraway seeds
1 teaspoon salt
1 cup dark rye flour
Approximately 5 cups unbleached all-purpose flour

Yield: 2 medium-size loaves

In a 6-quart mixing bowl, dissolve the yeast in the water. Add the remaining ingredients, mixing the salt with the flours, and work them into a dough.

Turn the dough out onto a lightly floured surface and knead it for 6 to 7 minutes, until the dough is smooth, elastic, and glossy.

Return the dough to the mixing bowl and cover it with a towel. Let the dough rise in a warm (75° F.) place for 50 minutes, or until doubled in bulk.

Divide the dough into 2 equal halves and shape each piece into an oblong loaf. Set the loaves on a baking sheet that has been greased with vegetable shortening. Cover the loaves with a towel and let them rise again for 50 minutes.

Bake in a preheated 375° F. oven for 45 minutes, or until golden brown. Remove the loaves from the baking sheet at once and allow them to cool on a wire rack.

Light Onion Rye

This is a Tyrolean bread, much loved by vacationers in Tyrol. The onions give this bread a pleasant unique flavor.

1 cake yeast
2 cups warm (110° F.) water
1 teaspoon vegetable oil
1 small onion, finely chopped
1 teaspoon salt
2 cups light rye flour
Approximately 4 cups unbleached all-purpose flour

Yield: 2 medium-size round loaves

In a 6-quart mixing bowl, dissolve the yeast in the water. Add the remaining ingredients, mixing the salt with the flours, and work them into a dough.

Turn the dough out onto a lightly floured surface and knead it for 6 to 7 minutes, until the dough is smooth, elastic, and glossy.

Return the dough to the mixing bowl and cover it with a towel. Let the dough rise in a warm (75° F.) place for 50 minutes, or until doubled in bulk.

Divide the dough into 2 equal halves and shape each piece into a round loaf. Set the loaves on a baking sheet that has been liberally dusted with cornmeal. Cover the loaves with a towel and let them rise again for 50 minutes.

Bake in a preheated 400° F. oven for 40 minutes, or until golden brown. Remove the loaves from the baking sheet at once and allow them to cool on a wire rack.

Dark Rye Onion Bread

This bread originated around the Oder River region between Poland and Czechoslovakia. Traditionally this bread is eaten with pork sausage and pilsner beer on the Slovakian side and with Polska kielbasa (Polish sausage) and Polish beer on the Polish side. Try it either way, or with any other combination you can think of.

1 cake yeast
2 cups warm (110° F.) water
1 teaspoon vegetable oil
1 teaspoon molasses
1 teaspoon finely chopped onion or dried onion flakes
2 teaspoons caraway seeds
1 teaspoon salt
2 cups dark rye flour
2 cups whole wheat flour
Approximately 2 cups unbleached all-purpose flour

Yield: 2 medium-size round loaves

In a 6-quart mixing bowl, dissolve the yeast in the water. Add the remaining ingredients, mixing the salt with the flours, and work them into a dough.

Turn the dough out onto a lightly floured surface and knead it for 6 to 7 minutes, until the dough is smooth, elastic, and somewhat glossy.

Return the dough to the mixing bowl and cover it with a towel. Let the dough rise in a warm (75° F.) place for 50 minutes, or until doubled in bulk.

Divide the dough into 2 equal halves and shape each piece into a round loaf. Set the loaves on a baking sheet that has been liberally dusted with cornmeal. Cover the loaves with a towel and let them rise again for 50 minutes.

Bake in a preheated 375° F. oven for 45 minutes, or until golden brown. Remove the loaves from the baking sheet at once and allow them to cool on a wire rack.

Pumpernickel Bread

In The Netherlands there is a province in the northern region called Groningen. Most of it is lush, fertile farmland where a lot of rye is grown. Its people are very independent, and they speak their own dialect. They love to eat a good dark coarse pumpernickel bread, like the one of this recipe, with smoked eel and dark beer.

1 cake yeast
2 cups warm (110° F.) water
1 teaspoon vegetable oil
2 teaspoons molasses
1 teaspoon caraway seeds
1 teaspoon salt
2 1/2 cups pumpernickel flour (rye meal) or dark rye flour
1 cup whole wheat flour
Approximately 2 1/2 cups unbleached flour

Yield: 2 medium-size round loaves

In a 6-quart mixing bowl, dissolve the yeast in the water. Add the remaining ingredients, mixing the salt with the flours, and work them into a dough.

Turn the dough out onto a lightly floured surface and knead it for 6 to 7 minutes, until the dough is smooth, elastic, and somewhat glossy.

Return the dough to the mixing bowl and cover it with a towel. Let the dough rise in a warm (75° F.) place for 45 minutes, or until doubled in bulk.

Divide the dough into 2 equal halves and shape each piece into a round loaf. Set the loaves on a baking sheet that has been liberally dusted with cornmeal. Cover the loaves with a towel and let them rise again for 45 minutes.

Bake in a preheated 400° F. oven for 45 minutes, or until golden brown. Remove the loaves from the baking sheet at once and allow them to cool on a wire rack.

Togenhoff Pumpernickel

Of Germanic origin, this rib-sticking bread is excellent for European-style open-face sandwiches. Slice it thin, spread with a good German mustard, and cover with Muenster cheese and thin slices of smoked ham. Have a stein of beer with it, close your eyes, and you will think you are at a sidewalk café in Bavaria, listening to the ompha-pah of a German band.

1 cake yeast
2 cups warm (110° F.) water
1 teaspoon vegetable oil
2 teaspoons molasses
1 teaspoon salt
1 cup pumpernickel (rye meal) or dark rye flour
1 cup whole wheat flour
Approximately 3 1/2 to 4 cups unbleached
  all-purpose flour

Yield: 2 medium-size round loaves

In a 6-quart mixing bowl, dissolve the yeast in the water. Add the remaining ingredients, mixing the salt with the flours, and work them into a dough.

Turn the dough out onto a lightly floured surface and knead it for 6 to 7 minutes, until the dough is smooth, elastic, and somewhat glossy.

Return the dough to the mixing bowl and cover it with a towel. Let the dough rise in a warm (75° F.) place for 1 hour, or until doubled in bulk.

Divide the dough into 2 equal halves and shape each piece into a round loaf. Set the loaves on a baking sheet that has been lightly greased with vegetable shortening. Cover the loaves with a towel and let them rise again for 50 minutes.

Bake in a preheated 400° F. oven for 45 minutes, or until golden brown. Remove the loaves from the baking sheet at once and allow them to cool on a wire rack.

Swedish Limpa

A good limpa *is a must for successful Scandinavian-style entertaining. Any smorgasbord should have three or four different kinds of breads and a* limpa *should always be among them. This is a very tasty bread that you can enjoy warm with butter and a good cup of coffee.*

1 cake yeast
2 cups warm (110° F.) water
2 teaspoons vegetable oil
2 teaspoons honey or sugar
1/2 teaspoon fennel seeds, crushed
1 teaspoon caraway seeds
Grated rind of 1 medium-size orange
1 teaspoon salt
2 cups light rye flour
Approximately 4 cups unbleached all-purpose
   flour

Yield: 2 medium-size loaves

In a 6-quart mixing bowl, dissolve the yeast in the water. Add the remaining ingredients, mixing the salt with the flours, and work them into a dough.

Turn the dough out onto a lightly floured surface and knead it for 6 to 7 minutes, until the dough is smooth, elastic, and somewhat glossy.

Return the dough to the mixing bowl and cover it with a towel. Let the dough rise in a warm (75° F.) place for 1 hour, or until doubled in bulk.

Divide the dough into 2 equal halves and shape each piece into an oblong loaf. Set the loaves on a baking sheet that has been lightly greased with vegetable shortening. Cover the loaves with a towel and let them rise again for 45 to 50 minutes.

Bake in a preheated 375° F. oven for 45 minutes, or until golden brown. Remove the loaves from the baking sheet at once and allow them to cool on a wire rack.

Finnish Limpa

One of the things that Scandinavian lands have in
common is limpa. The name of this bread is the
same, yet each nation has its own distinct version.
This Finnish limpa is delicious with a mild cheese
and wine.

1 cake yeast
4 teaspoons molasses
2 cups warm (110° F.) water
1 teaspoon vegetable oil
Grated rind of 1 medium-size orange
1/2 teaspoon fennel seeds, crushed
Pinch ground cardamom
1 teaspoon salt
2 1/2 cups dark rye flour
Approximately 3 1/2 cups unbleached
  all-purpose flour

Yield: 2 medium-size loaves

In a 6-quart mixing bowl, dissolve the yeast and
the molasses in the water. Add the remaining ingredients, mixing the salt with the flours, and work
them into a dough.

Turn the dough out onto a lightly floured surface and knead it for 6 to 7 minutes, until the dough
is smooth, elastic, and somewhat glossy.

Return the dough to the mixing bowl and cover
it with a towel. Let the dough rise in a warm (75°
F.) place for 50 minutes, or until doubled in bulk.

Divide the dough into 2 equal halves and shape
each piece into an oblong loaf. Set the loaves on
a baking sheet that has been lightly greased with
vegetable shortening. Cover the loaves with a towel
and let them rise again for 50 minutes.

Bake in a preheated 375° F. oven for 50 minutes,
or until golden brown. Remove the loaves from the
baking sheet at once and allow them to cool on
a wire rack.

Rye Mush Bread

This old-fashioned Dutch rye bread will stay fresh for several days. The recipe makes a moist, hearty, compact bread that is delicious with Gouda cheese and Dutch beer.

2 cups water
1 cup light rye flour
1 teaspoon caraway seeds
1 cake yeast
2 teaspoons vegetable oil
2 teaspoons sorghum or sugar
1 teaspoon salt
Approximately 5 cups unbleached all-purpose flour

Yield: 2 round loaves

Bring the water to a slow boil. Add the rye flour and the caraway seeds. Stirring constantly, boil for 1 minute. Do not overcook. Let cool to about 110° F. Transfer to a 6-quart mixing bowl and add the yeast. Mix well. Let stand for 5 minutes. Then add the remaining ingredients, mixing the salt with the remaining flour, and work into a dough.

Turn the dough out onto a lightly floured surface and knead it for 6 to 7 minutes, until the dough is smooth, elastic, and glossy.

Return the dough to the mixing bowl and cover with a towel. Let rise in a warm (75° F.) place for 1 hour, or until doubled in bulk.

Divide the dough into 2 equal halves and shape each into a round loaf. Set on a baking sheet that has been liberally dusted with cornmeal. Cover with a towel and let them rise again for 50 minutes.

Bake in a preheated 400° F. oven for 10 minutes. Then reduce the oven temperature to 375° F. and bake for 35 minutes more, or until the loaves are golden brown. Remove from the baking sheet at once and cool on a wire rack.

Dutch Steamed Bread

This is a very old and very unique Dutch recipe. In Holland, this bread is called Jan in de Zak *or "Joe in a Bag." It is a dark loaf that is moist and will stay fresh for a long time. Slice it very thin and serve it with a sharp cheese or smoked ham.*

1 cake yeast
2 cups warm (110° F.) water
4 teaspoons molasses
2 teaspoons sorghum or sugar
1 tablespoon caraway seeds
2 cups whole wheat flour
1 1/4 teaspoons salt
Approximately 4 cups light rye flour

Yield: 1 large loaf

In a 6-quart mixing bowl, dissolve the yeast in the water. Add the remaining ingredients, working them into a dough.

Turn the dough out onto a lightly floured surface and knead it for 6 to 7 minutes, until the dough is smooth, elastic, and glossy.

Place the dough in a well-greased 3-pound coffee can. Securely tie a double piece of aluminum foil over the open end of the coffee can, closing it tightly. Place the coffe can in a deep pan of warm (110° F.) water. Completely immerse the can in the water. Now bring the water to a slow boil and let it boil for 3 1/2 hours (the bread will rise while the water comes to a boil).

Remove the pan from the heat. Very carefully pour out the hot water and remove the coffee can from the pan. Remove the loaf from the coffee can. Set the loaf, standing on one end, on a lightly greased baking sheet.

Bake in a preheated 375° F. oven for 1 hour. Remove from the baking sheet and cool on a wire rack.

Cheese Rye Bread

In Greece this bread often makes a complete meal. They like it thickly sliced, spread with plenty of butter, and served with lentil soup. The flavor of the cheese comes through very distinctly—vary the cheese, and you'll vary the flavor.

1 cake yeast
2 cups warm (110° F.) water
3/4 cup shredded sharp cheese
1 teaspoon salt
2 cups light rye flour
Approximately 4 cups unbleached all-purpose
  flour

Yield: 2 medium-size round loaves

In a 6-quart mixing bowl, dissolve the yeast in the water. Add the remaining ingredients, mixing the salt with the flours, and work them into a dough.

Turn the dough out onto a lightly floured surface and knead it for 6 to 7 minutes, until the dough is smooth, elastic, and somewhat glossy.

Return the dough to the mixing bowl and cover it with a towel. Let the dough rise in a warm (75° F.) place for 50 minutes, or until doubled in bulk.

Divide the dough into 2 equal halves and shape each piece into a round loaf. Set the loaves on a baking sheet that has been liberally dusted with cornmeal. Cover the loaves with a towel and let them rise again for 50 minutes.

Bake in a preheated 375° F. oven for 45 minutes, or until golden brown. Remove the loaves from the baking sheet at once and allow them to cool on a wire rack.

Nordic Ham Bread

This is a delicious bread from northern Europe.
It makes very good sandwiches.

1 cake yeast
2 cups warm (110° F.) water
2 teaspoons molasses
6 ounces Danish-style ham, finely chopped
1 tablespoon caraway seeds
1 teaspoon salt
1 cup dark rye flour
Approximately 5 cups unbleached all-purpose
    flour

Yield: 2 medium-size loaves

In a 6-quart mixing bowl, dissolve the yeast in the water. Add the remaining ingredients, mixing the salt with the flours, and work them into a dough.

Turn the dough out onto a lightly floured surface and knead it for 6 to 7 minutes, until the dough is smooth, elastic, and somewhat glossy.

Return the dough to the mixing bowl and cover it with a towel. Let the dough rise in a warm (75° F.) place for 1 hour, or until doubled in bulk.

Divide the dough into 2 equal halves and shape each piece into an oblong loaf. Set the loaves on a baking sheet that has been lightly greased with vegetable shortening. Cover the loaves with a towel and let them rise again for 50 minutes.

Bake in a preheated 375° F. oven for 45 minutes, or until golden brown. Remove the loaves from the baking sheet at once and allow them to cool on a wire rack.

Dutch Kraut Bread

From the border region of Holland and Germany comes this recipe for a very tart, moist bread. It is very good for European open-face sandwiches with Gouda cheese or thinly sliced ham.

1 cake yeast
2 cups warm (110° F.) water
1 cup light rye flour
1/4 cup drained chopped sauerkraut
1 tablespoon caraway seeds
1 teaspoon salt
Approximately 5 cups unbleached all-purpose flour

Yield: 2 medium-size round loaves

In a 6-quart mixing bowl, dissolve half the yeast in 1 cup of the water. Add the rye flour. Mix well. Let this ferment for 3 1/2 hours in a warm (75° F.) place. Then add the rest of the yeast and the remaining 1 cup warm water. Mix well. Add all the remaining ingredients, mixing the salt with the remaining flour, and work them into a dough.

Turn the dough out onto a lightly floured surface and knead it for 6 to 7 minutes, until the dough is smooth, elastic, and glossy.

Return the dough to the mixing bowl and cover with a towel. Let rise in a warm (75° F.) place for 1 hour, or until doubled in bulk.

Divide the dough into 2 equal halves and shape each into a round loaf. Set on a baking sheet that has been liberally dusted with cornmeal. Cover with a towel and let rise again for 50 minutes.

Bake in a preheated 400° F. oven for 40 minutes, or until golden brown. Remove the loaves from the baking sheet at once and allow them to cool on a wire rack.

Roggen Loaf

ထထထထထထထထထထထထထထထထထထထထထထထထထထထထထထထထ

Roggen *means rye in German and Dutch. This light rye bread has a unique flavor from the sauerkraut juice. It's an excellent bread for Reuben sandwiches.*

1 cake yeast
1 1/2 cups warm (110° F.) water
1 cup light rye flour
1/2 cup warm (110° F.) sauerkraut juice
2 teaspoons molasses
1 teaspoon caraway seeds
Approximately 5 cups unbleached all-purpose
   flour

Yield: 2 medium-size round loaves

In a 6-quart mixing bowl, dissolve the yeast in the water. Add the rye flour. Mix well. Let this ferment for 30 minutes in a warm (75° F.) place. Then add the remaining ingredients and work them into a dough.

Turn the dough out onto a lightly floured surface and knead it for 6 to 7 minutes, until the dough is smooth, elastic, and glossy.

Return the dough to the mixing bowl and cover it with a towel. Let the dough rise in a warm (75° F.) place for 1 hour, or until doubled in bulk.

Divide the dough into 2 equal halves and shape each piece into a round loaf. Set the loaves on a baking sheet that has been liberally dusted with cornmeal. Cover the loaves with a towel and let them rise again for 50 minutes.

Bake in a preheated 400° F. oven for 40 minutes, or until golden brown. Remove the loaves from the baking sheet at once and allow them to cool on a wire rack.

Scheele's All-Rye Bread

I developed this recipe at the request of a good friend who was allergic to wheat. This is a naturally heavy bread. It is delicious when sliced thin and served with a very sharp cheese and Dutch beer.

1 cake yeast
2 cups warm (110° F.) water
2 teaspoons molasses
2 teaspoons caraway seeds
1 teaspoon salt
Approximately 6 cups light rye flour

Yield: 1 medium-size loaf

In a 6-quart mixing bowl, dissolve the yeast in the water. Add the remaining ingredients, mixing the salt with the flour, and work them into a dough.

Turn the dough out onto a lightly floured surface and knead it for 4 to 5 minutes. Do not overknead.

After kneading the dough, shape it into 1 round loaf. Set the loaf on a baking sheet that has been liberally dusted with cornmeal. Cover it with a towel and let it rise in a warm (75° F.) place for 1 hour, or until it has increased by 50 percent of its original size.

Bake in a preheated 375° F. oven for 1 hour. Remove the loaf from the baking sheet at once and allow it to cool on a wire rack.

Dark Russian Rye

∞∞

From the Baltic republics of the Soviet Union comes this robust, hearty rye bread. It is traditionally eaten with butter and herring, or as an accompaniment for cabbage soup spiced with caraway seeds.

1 1/4 cakes yeast (or 4 teaspoons dry yeast)
2 cups warm (110° F.) water
1 3/4 cups dark rye flour
2 teaspoons molasses
1 tablespoon caraway seeds
1 teaspoon salt
2 cups whole wheat flour
Approximately 2 cups unbleached all-purpose flour

Yield: 2 medium-size loaves

In a small crock, dissolve 1/4 cake of the yeast (or 1 teaspoon dry yeast) in 1/4 cup of the water. Add 1/4 cup of the rye flour. Mix well. Let this ferment for 24 hours in a warm (75° F.) place.

The next day, add the remaining 1 cake yeast (or 3 teaspoons dry yeast), 3/4 cups warm water, and 1/2 cup dark rye flour. Mix well and let this ferment for 3 1/2 hours in a warm (75° F.) place.

Place the fermented mixture in a 6-quart mixing bowl, and add the remaining 1 cup water, the remaining 1 cup dark rye flour, and all the other ingredients, mixing the salt with the flours. Mix well, working it into a dough.

Turn the dough out onto a lightly floured surface and knead it for 6 to 7 minutes, until the dough is smooth, elastic, and somewhat glossy.

Return the dough to the mixing bowl and cover it with a towel. Let the dough rise in a warm (75° F.) place for 20 minutes.

Divide the dough into 2 equal halves and shape each piece into a round loaf. Cover the loaves with a towel and let them rise for 20 minutes. Then reshape the round loaves into oblong loaves. Set the loaves on a baking sheet that has been liberally dusted with cornmeal. Cover the loaves with a towel and let them rise again for 40 minutes.

Bake in a preheated 400° F. oven for 40 minutes, or until golden brown. Remove the loaves from the baking sheet at once and allow them to cool on a wire rack.

Dutch-Style Sourdough Rye

∞∞

Similar to the Dutch Sourdough White Bread, this delicious sourdough rye bread is chewy on the inside and crusty on the outside. It has a slightly tangy flavor and makes excellent European-style open-face sandwiches.

1 1/4 cakes yeast (or 4 teaspoons dry yeast)
2 cups warm (110° F.) water
1 teaspoon salt
2 1/4 cups dark rye flour
1 cup whole wheat flour
Approximately 2 3/4 cups unbleached
   all-purpose flour

Yield: 2 medium-size loaves

In a small crock, dissolve 1/4 cake of the yeast (or 1 teaspoon dry yeast) in 1/4 cup of the water. Add 1/4 cup of the rye flour. Mix well. Let this ferment in a warm (75° F.) place for 24 hours.

The next day, add the remaining 1 cake yeast (or 3 teaspoons dry yeast), 1 cup warm water, and 1 cup dark rye flour. Mix well and let this ferment in a warm (75° F.) place for 3 1/2 hours.

Place the fermented mixture in a 6-quart mixing bowl, and add the remaining 3/4 cup warm water, 1 cup rye flour, and all the other ingredients, mixing the salt with the flours. Mix all the ingredients well and work them into a dough.

Turn the dough out onto a lightly floured surface and knead it for 6 to 7 minutes, until the dough is smooth, elastic, and somewhat glossy.

Return the dough to the mixing bowl and cover it with a towel. Let the dough rise in a warm (75° F.) place for 20 minutes.

Divide the dough into 2 equal halves and shape each piece into a round loaf. Cover the loaves with a towel and let them rise for 20 minutes. Then reshape the round loaves into oblong loaves. Set the loaves on a baking sheet that has been liberally dusted with cornmeal. Cover the loaves with a towel and let them rise again for 40 minutes.

Bake in a preheated 400° F. oven for 40 minutes, or until golden brown. Remove the loaves from the baking sheet at once and allow them to cool on a wire rack.

Jewish Rye Bread

The great variety of Jewish baking evolved as Jews traveled from country to country, adopting and adapting traditions of the host country. This is the classic rye bread that is found in many delicatessens. Jewish rye bread is a delicious bread very similar to Polish rye bread, which is given as a variation.

1 1/4 cakes yeast (or 4 teaspoons dry yeast)
2 cups warm (110° F.) water
2 cups light rye flour
1 teaspoon molasses
1 tablespoon caraway seeds
1 teaspoon salt
Approximately 4 cups unbleached
   all-purpose flour

Yield: 2 medium-size loaves

In a small crock or glass jar, dissolve 1/4 cake of the yeast (or 1 teaspoon dry yeast) in 1/4 cup of the water. Add 1/4 cup of the rye flour. Mix well. Let this ferment in a warm (75° F.) place for 24 hours.

The next day, add the remaining 1 cake yeast (or 3 teaspoons dry yeast), 3/4 cup warm water, and 3/4 cup light rye flour. Mix well and let this ferment in a warm (75° F.) place for 3 1/2 hours.

Place the fermented mixture in a 6-quart mixing bowl, and add the remaining 1 cup warm water, 1 cup light rye flour, and all the other ingredients, mixing the salt with the all-purpose flour. Mix well, working it into a dough.

Turn the dough out onto a lightly floured surface and knead it for 6 to 7 minutes, until the dough is smooth, elastic, and somewhat glossy.

Return the dough to the mixing bowl and cover it with a towel. Let the dough rise in a warm (75° F.) place for 20 minutes.

Divide the dough into 2 equal halves and shape

each piece into a round loaf. Cover the loaves with a towel and let them rise for 20 minutes. Then reshape the round loaves into oblong loaves. Set the loaves on a baking sheet that has been liberally dusted with cornmeal. Cover the loaves with a towel and let them rise again for 40 minutes.

Bake in a preheated 400° F. oven for 40 minutes, or until golden brown. Remove the loaves from the baking sheet at once and allow them to cool on a wire rack.

Variation

Polish Rye. Substitute dark rye flour for the light rye flour.

Old Dutch Rye

This is a very old recipe, and it makes a delicious compact loaf that is a naturally fermented, so no yeast is required. It goes very well with cheese and beer.

1 cup farm fresh milk (do not substitute milk that has been pasteurized or homogenized)
1 cup dark rye flour
1 cup warm (110° F.) water
1 teaspoon caraway seeds
1 teaspoon salt
Approximately 5 cups unbleached all-purpose flour

Yield: 2 small round loaves

In a small crock or glass jar, mix the milk and 1/2 cup of the rye flour. Ferment in a warm (75° F.) place for 72 hours, until bubbly.

Then add the remaining 1/2 cup dark rye flour. Mix well, and let this ferment in a warm place overnight or for 12 hours.

The next day, place this fermented mixture in a 6-quart mixing bowl, and add the remaining ingredients, mixing the salt with the flour. Mix well, working it into a dough. Turn the dough out onto a lightly floured surface and knead it for 4 minutes. Do not overknead.

Immediately divide the dough into 2 equal halves and shape each piece into a round loaf. Set the loaves on a baking sheet that has been liberally dusted with cornmeal. Cover the loaves with a towel and let them rise in a warm (75° F.) place for 8 hours, or until the volume of dough has increased by 50 percent.

Bake in a preheated 375° F. oven for 45 minutes, or until golden brown. Cool on a wire rack.

5
Sweet and Specialty Breads

During the work week we baked mostly whole grain breads at my grandfather's bakery, as it was customary in Holland. Sweet breads were considered a luxury, reserved for Sunday and special occasions.

Since the bakery was closed on Sunday, most of the sweet breads were baked on Saturday. On this day the bakery had a special atmosphere— created not only by the anticipation of a rest day, but also by the special aromas of the different spices used, the candied fruit, raisins, and so on. Weddings and special occasions in the community also contributed to a special feeling of excitement among the bakers as they always had a part in such celebrations. The town was small and the people had close bonds of friendship with one another.

Baking sweet breads always brought us an extra dose of contentment and satisfaction, knowing that the fruits of our labor were very much appreciated by the people on their special days.

Citus Loaf

From southern Europe comes this choice recipe for a zesty, citrus-flavored bread that will delight your family at the breakfast table.

1 cake yeast
2 cups warm (110° F.) skim milk
1 tablespoon vegetable oil
4 teaspoons honey or sugar
3 eggs, at room temperature, lightly beaten
Grated rind of 1 medium-size orange
Grated rind of 1 medium size lemon
1/2 cup finely chopped citron
1 teaspoon salt
Approximately 6 cups unbleached all-purpose flour

Yield: 2 medium-size round loaves

In a 6-quart mixing bowl, dissolve the yeast in the milk. Add the remaining ingredients, mixing the salt with the flour, and work them into a dough.

Turn the dough out onto a lightly floured surface and knead it for 6 to 7 minutes, until the dough is smooth, elastic, and somewhat glossy.

Return the dough to the mixing bowl and cover it with a towel. Let the dough rise in a warm (75° F.) place for 1 hour, or until doubled in bulk.

Divide the dough into 2 equal halves and shape each piece into a round loaf. Set the loaves on a baking sheet that has been lightly greased with vegetable shortening. Cover the loaves with a towel and let them rise again for 55 minutes.

Bake in a preheated 375° F. oven for 40 to 45 minutes, or until golden brown. Remove the loaves from the baking sheet at once and allow them to cool on a wire rack.

Fragrant Anise Bread

This delightful bread combines the flavors of citrus and anise.

1 cake yeast
2 cups warm (110° F.) milk
1 tablespoon vegetable oil
4 teaspoons honey or sugar
2 eggs, at room temperature, lightly beaten
Grated rind of 1 medium-size orange
Grated rind of 1 medium-size lemon
1 1/2 teaspoons anise seeds, crushed
1 teaspoon salt
Approximately 6 cups unbleached all-purpose
  flour

Yield: 2 medium-size round loaves

In a 6-quart mixing bowl, dissolve the yeast in the milk. Add the remaining ingredients, mixing the salt with the flour, and work them into a dough.

Turn the dough out onto a lightly floured surface and knead it for 6 to 7 minutes, until the dough is smooth, elastic, and somewhat glossy.

Return the dough to the mixing bowl and cover it with a towel. Let the dough rise in a warm (75° F.) place for 1 hour, or until doubled in bulk.

Divide the dough into 2 equal halves and shape each piece into a round loaf. Set the loaves on a baking sheet that has been lightly greased with vegetable shortening. Cover the loaves with a towel and let them rise again for 50 minutes.

Bake in a preheated 350° F. oven for 45 minutes, or until golden brown. Remove the loaves from the baking sheet at once and allow them to cool on a wire rack.

Sweet Greek Bread

This cake-like bread is great for an afternoon of entertaining with cheese, fruit, coffee, and, for a grand finish, an anisette cordial.

1 cake yeast
2 cups warm (110° F.) milk
2 teaspoons vegetable oil
2 tablespoons honey
4 egg yolks, at room temperature
1 teaspoon anise seeds
1 teaspoon salt
Approximately 6 cups unbleached all-purpose flour

Yield: 2 medium-size round loaves

In a 6-quart mixing bowl, dissolve the yeast in the milk. Add the remaining ingredients, mixing the salt with the flour, and work them into a dough.

Turn the dough out onto a lightly floured surface and knead it for 6 to 7 minutes, until the dough is smooth, elastic, and somewhat glossy.

Return the dough to the mixing bowl and cover it with a towel. Let the dough rise in a warm (75° F.) place for 1 hour, or until doubled in bulk.

Divide the dough into 2 equal halves and shape each piece into a round loaf. Set the loaves on a baking sheet that has been lightly greased with vegetable shortening. Cover the loaves with a towel and let them rise again for 55 minutes.

Bake in a preheated 350° F. oven for 40 minutes, or until golden brown. Remove the loaves from the baking sheet at once and allow them to cool on a wire rack.

Greek Fruit Bread

A sweet, fruited bread, try serving it with a mild cheese, such as mild brick or Monterey jack. Or have it the Greek way, with feta cheese and coffee.

1 cake yeast
2 cups warm (110° F.) milk
2 teaspoons vegetable oil
5 teaspoons honey
3 egg yolks, at room temperature
1/2 cup chopped dried apricots
1/2 cup dried currants
1/2 cup chopped nuts
Grated rind of 1 medium-size lemon
1 teaspoon anise seeds
1 teaspoon salt
Approximately 6 cups unbleached all-purpose flour

Yield: 2 medium-size round loaves

In a 6-quart mixing bowl, dissolve the yeast in the milk. Add the remaining ingredients, mixing the salt with the flour, and work them into a dough.

Turn the dough onto a lightly floured surface and knead it for 6 to 7 minutes, until the dough is smooth, elastic, and somewhat glossy.

Return the dough to the mixing bowl and cover it with a towel. Let the dough rise in a warm (75° F.) place for 1 hour, or until doubled in bulk.

Divide the dough into 2 equal halves and shape each piece into a round loaf. Set the loaves on a baking sheet that has been lightly greased with vegetable shortening. Cover the loaves with a towel and let them rise again for 50 minutes.

Bake in a preheated 350° F. oven for 45 minutes, or until golden brown. Remove the loaves from the baking sheet at once and allow them to cool on a wire rack.

Cinnamon Almond Loaf

This is a rich-tasting bread. It makes exquisite toast for breakfast, a special treat for a Sunday brunch.

Bread

1 cake yeast
2 cups warm (110° F.) milk
2 teaspoons vegetable oil
4 teaspoons honey or sugar
4 egg yolks, at room temperature
1/2 cup chopped almonds
1 teaspoon pure almond extract
1/2 teaspoon cinnamon
1 teaspoon salt
Approximately 6 cups unbleached all-purpose flour

Glaze

1 egg white
Sliced almonds

Yield: 2 medium-size loaves

In a 6-quart mixing bowl, dissolve the yeast in the milk. Add the remaining ingredients, mixing the salt with the flour, and work them into a dough.

Turn the dough onto a lightly floured surface and knead it for 6 to 7 minutes, until the dough is smooth, elastic, and somewhat glossy.

Return the dough to the mixing bowl and cover it with a towel. Let the dough rise in a warm (75° F.) place for 1 hour, or until doubled in bulk.

Divide the dough into 2 equal halves and shape each piece into an oblong loaf. Set the loaves on a baking sheet that has been lightly greased with vegetable shortening. Cover the loaves with a towel and let them rise again for 1 hour. Brush the loaves with the egg white and sprinkle them with the sliced almonds.

Bake in a preheated 350° F. oven for 50 minutes, or until golden brown. Remove the loaves from the baking sheet at once and allow them to cool on a wire rack.

Frisian Ginger Bread

This spicy bread came from the small West Frisian Islands in the North Sea. The flavor is reminiscent of gingersnaps.

1 cake yeast
2 cups warm (110° F.) milk
Approximately 6 cups unbleached all-purpose
   flour
1 teaspoon vegetable oil
1/4 cup light molasses
1 egg, at room temperature, lightly beaten
1/4 teaspoon ginger
Pinch mace
Pinch ground cloves
1 teaspoon salt

Yield: 2 medium-size loaves

In a 6-quart mixing bowl, dissolve half the yeast in 1 cup of the milk. Add 1 cup of the flour. Mix well. Let this ferment in a warm (75° F.) place for 3 1/2 hours. Then add the rest of the yeast and the milk. Mix well. Add the remaining ingredients, mixing the salt with the flour, and work them into a dough.

Turn the dough onto a lightly floured surface and knead it for 6 to 7 minutes, until the dough is smooth, elastic, and somewhat glossy.

Return the dough to the mixing bowl and cover with a towel. Let rise in a warm (75° F.) place for 1 hour, or until doubled in bulk.

Divide the dough into 2 equal halves and shape each piece into an oblong loaf. Set the loaves on a baking sheet that has been lightly greased with vegetable shortening. Cover the loaves with a towel and let them rise again for 50 minutes.

Bake in a preheated 375° F. oven for 40 minutes, or until golden brown. Remove from the baking sheet at once and cool on a wire rack.

Yorkshire Breakfast Bread

This is a rich breakfast bread, delicious with butter, marmalade, and some good English tea. It is also quite lovely at tea time.

1 cake yeast
2 cups warm (110° F.) milk
2 teaspoons vegetable oil
1 tablespoon honey or sugar
3 egg yolks, at room temperature
1/2 cup dried currants
1/2 cup raisins
Grated rind of 1 lemon
Grated rind of 1 orange
Pinch nutmeg
1 teaspoon salt
Approximately 6 cups unbleached all-purpose flour

Yield: 2 medium-size loaves

In a 6-quart mixing bowl, dissolve the yeast in the milk. Add the remaining ingredients, mixing the salt with the flour, and work them into a dough.

Turn the dough onto a lightly floured surface and knead it for 6 to 7 minutes, until the dough is smooth, elastic, and somewhat glossy.

Return the dough to the mixing bowl and cover it with a towel. Let the dough rise in a warm (75° F.) place for 1 hour, or until doubled in bulk.

Divide the dough into 2 equal halves and shape each piece into an oblong loaf. Set the loaves on a baking sheet that has been lightly greased with vegetable shortening. Cover the loaves with a towel and let them rise again for 55 minutes.

Bake in a preheated 350° F. oven for 45 minutes, or until golden brown. Remove the loaves from the baking sheet at once and allow them to cool on a wire rack.

Date Walnut Loaf

This is a British recipe for a fruited bread that is delicious for breakfast with tea and marmalade.

1 cake yeast
2 cups warm (110° F.) water
Approximately 6 cups unbleached all-purpose
  flour
2 teaspoons vegetable oil
1 tablespoon honey or sugar
2 eggs, at room temperature, lightly beaten
1/2 cup chopped dates
1/2 cup chopped walnuts
Pinch cinnamon
1 teaspoon salt

Yield: 2 medium-size loaves

In a 6-quart mixing bowl, dissolve half the yeast in 1 cup of the water. Add 1 cup of the flour. Mix well. Let this ferment in a warm (75° F.) place for 3 1/2 hours. Then add the rest of the yeast and the water. Mix well. Add the remaining ingredients, mixing the salt with the flour, and work them into a dough.

Turn the dough onto a lightly floured surface and knead it for 6 to 7 minutes, until the dough is smooth, elastic, and somewhat glossy.

Return the dough to the mixing bowl and cover with a towel. Let rise in a warm (75° F.) place for 1 hour, or until doubled in bulk.

Divide the dough into 2 equal halves and shape each piece into an oblong loaf. Set on a baking sheet that has been lightly greased with vegetable shortening. Cover the loaves with a towel and let them rise again for 50 minutes.

Bake in a preheated 375° F. oven for 45 minutes, or until golden brown. Remove from the baking sheet at once and cool on a wire rack.

Dutch Prune Bread

∞∞

This is a delicious bread that we baked in Holland mostly for the weekends. We usually had it for breakfast along with other different kinds of breads. If you like the taste of prunes, you'll like this sweet, spicy bread.

1 cake yeast
2 cups warm (110° F.) milk
1 tablespoon vegetable oil
4 teaspoons honey or sugar
3 eggs, at room temperature, lightly beaten
1 cup chopped soft pitted prunes
Pinch cinnamon
Pinch allspice
1 teaspoon salt
Approximately 6 cups unbleached all-purpose
   flour

Yield: 2 medium-size loaves

In a 6-quart mixing bowl, dissolve the yeast in the milk. Add the remaining ingredients, mixing the salt with the flour, and work them into a dough.

Turn the dough onto a lightly floured surface and knead it for 6 to 7 minutes, until the dough is smooth, elastic, and somewhat glossy.

Return the dough to the mixing bowl and cover it with a towel. Let the dough rise in a warm (75° F.) place for 1 hour, or until doubled in bulk.

Divide the dough into 2 equal halves and shape each piece into an oblong loaf. Set the loaves on a baking sheet that has been lightly greased with vegetable shortening. Cover the loaves with a towel and let them rise again for 50 minutes.

Bake in a preheated 350° F. oven for 40 minutes, or until golden brown. Remove the loaves from the baking sheet at once and allow them to cool on a wire rack.

Coffee Bread

Many people in Europe still like to take their time, just like in the olden days, to savor coffee or tea with their friends in the afternoons as a respite from the daily work routine. And if they have with it a slice of a sweet bread like this, so much the better.

1 cake yeast
1 cup warm (110° F.) milk
Approximately 6 cups unbleached all-purpose flour
1 cup warm (110° F.) strong coffee
1 teaspoon vegetable oil
1 tablespoon honey or sugar
2 eggs, at room temperature, lightly beaten
1/2 cup raisins
Grated rind of 1 medium-size lemon
1 teaspoon brandy
Pinch cinnamon
Pinch allspice
1 teaspoon salt

Yield: 2 medium-size loaves

In a 6-quart mixing bowl, dissolve half the yeast in the milk. Add 1 cup of the flour. Mix well. Let this ferment in a warm (75° F.) place for 3 1/2 hours. Then add the rest of the yeast and the coffee. Mix well. Add the remaining ingredients, mixing the salt with the remaining flour, and work them into a dough.

Turn the dough onto a lightly floured surface and knead it for 6 to 7 minutes, until the dough is smooth, elastic, and somewhat glossy.

Return the dough to the mixing bowl and cover with a towel. Let rise in a warm (75° F.) place for 1 hour, or until doubled in bulk.

Divide the dough into 2 equal halves and shape each piece into an oblong loaf. Set the loaves on a baking sheet that has been lightly greased with vegetable shortening. Cover the loaves with a towel and let them rise again for 50 minutes.

Bake in a preheated 375° F. oven for 35 to 40 minutes, or until golden brown. Remove the loaves from the baking sheet at once and allow them to cool on a wire rack.

Spiced French Coffee Bread

This comes from Southern France, specifically the Armagnac district, which is famous for its fine brandy. Many of the region's breads are flavored with it. You can substitute any good brandy.

1/2 cup raisins
1 tablespoon brandy
1 cake yeast
1 cup warm (110° F.) milk
1 cup warm (110° F.) strong coffee
2 teaspoons vegetable oil
4 teaspoons honey
3 eggs, at room temperature, lightly beaten
1/2 cup chopped nuts
Grated rind of 1 lemon
Pinch cinnamon
Pinch allspice
Pinch ground cloves
1 teaspoon salt
Approximately 6 cups unbleached all-purpose
  flour

Yield: 2 medium-size loaves

Marinate the raisins in the brandy for 15 minutes. In a 6-quart mixing bowl, dissolve the yeast in the milk. Add the marinated raisins and remaining ingredients, mixing the salt with the flour, and work them into a dough.

Turn the dough onto a lightly floured surface and knead it for 6 to 7 minutes, until the dough is smooth, elastic, and somewhat glossy.

Return the dough to the mixing bowl and cover with a towel. Let the dough rise in a warm (75° F.) place for 1 hour, or until doubled in bulk.

Divide the dough into 2 equal halves and shape each into an oblong loaf. Set on a baking sheet that has been lightly greased with vegetable shortening. Cover the loaves with a towel and let them rise again for 50 minutes.

Bake in a preheated 350° F. oven for 45 minutes, or until golden brown. Remove the loaves from the baking sheet at once and allow them to cool on a wire rack.

Dutch Treat

Here's a bread with the flavor of apple pie.

Bread

1 cake yeast
2 cups warm (110° F.) milk
2 teaspoons vegetable oil
2 teaspoons honey or sugar
2 eggs, at room temperature, lightly beaten
1 teaspoon salt
Approximately 6 cups unbleached
  all-purpose flour

Filling

Milk
2 apples, peeled and chopped
5 teaspoons brown sugar
Pinch cinnamon
Pinch ground cloves
Pinch mace

Yield: 2 medium-size loaves

In a 6-quart mixing bowl, dissolve the yeast in the milk. Add the remaining bread ingredients, mixing the salt with the flour, and work them into a dough.

Turn the dough onto a lightly floured surface and knead it for 6 to 7 minutes, until the dough is smooth, elastic, and somewhat glossy.

Return the dough to the mixing bowl and cover it with a towel. Let the dough rise in a warm (75° F.) place for 1 hour, or until doubled in bulk.

Divide the dough into 2 equal halves. With a rolling pin, roll each piece into a rectangle 11 inches long by 6 inches wide, and about 1/2 inch thick. Brush the surface of each rectangle with a little milk. Combine the apples, brown sugar, and spices and mix well. Divide the filling mixture in half, and sprinkle half over each rectangle of dough. Starting at the narrow end, roll each rectangle of dough as you would a jelly roll. Set the loaves seam side down on a lightly greased baking sheet. Cover the loaves with a towel and let them rise again for 1 hour.

Bake in a preheated 350° F. oven for 50 minutes, or until golden brown. Remove the loaves from the baking sheet at once and allow them to cool on a wire rack.

Dutch Cinnamon Swirl

Bread

1 cake yeast
2 cups warm (110° F.) skim milk
1 tablespoon vegetable oil
1 tablespoon sorghum or sugar
3 eggs, at room temperature, lightly beaten
1 teaspoon salt
Approximately 6 cups unbleached all-purpose
   flour

Filling

Melted butter
1 teaspoon cinnamon
5 teaspoons brown sugar
1/2 cup raisins

Yield: 1 large loaf

In a 6-quart bowl, dissolve the yeast in the milk. Add the remaining bread ingredients, mixing the salt with the flour, and work into a dough.

Turn the dough onto a lightly floured surface and knead it for 6 to 7 minutes, until the dough is smooth, elastic, and somewhat glossy.

Return the dough to the mixing bowl and cover with a towel. Let rise in a warm (75° F.) place for 1 hour, or until doubled in bulk.

With a rolling pin, roll the dough into a rectangle 20 inches long by 10 inches wide, and approximately 1 inch thick. Brush it with a little melted butter. Combine the cinnamon, brown sugar, and raisins and sprinkle this filling over the dough. Starting at the narrow end, roll the dough as you would a jelly roll. Set the loaf seam side down on a lightly greased baking sheet. Cover it with a towel and let rise again for 50 minutes.

Bake in a preheated 350° F. oven for 45 to 50 minutes, or until golden brown. Remove from the baking sheet at once and cool on a wire rack.

Hungarian Poppy Seed Bread

Bread
1 cake yeast
2 cups warm (110° F.) milk
Approximately 6 cups unbleached all-purpose
  flour
1 tablespoon vegetable oil
1 tablespoon honey or sugar
3 eggs, at room temperature, lightly beaten
1 teaspoon salt

Filling

4 teaspoons milk
4 teaspoons sugar
1/2 cup raisins
1/2 cup chopped pecans
1 cup ground poppy seeds
Grated rind of 1 medium-size lemon

Yield: 1 large loaf

In a 6-quart bowl, dissolve half the yeast in 1 cup milk. Add 1 cup flour. Mix well. Ferment in a warm (75° F.) place for 3 1/2 hours. Add the rest of the yeast and the milk. Mix well. Add the remaining bread ingredients, mixing the salt with the flour, and work into a dough. Turn onto a lightly floured surface and knead for 6 to 7 minutes, until the dough is smooth and elastic.

Return the dough to the mixing bowl and cover with a towel. Let rise in a warm (75° F.) place for 1 hour, or until doubled in bulk.

Roll the dough flat and make a rectangle 24 inches by 20 inches. Combine the filling ingredients and mix well. Spread over the dough. Starting at the narrow end, roll up the rectangle as you would a jelly roll. Seal the ends.

Set seam side down on a baking sheet that has been lightly greased with vegetable shortening. Cover with a towel and let rise again, until the bulk has increased by 60 to 70 percent.

Bake in a preheated 375° F. oven for 1 hour, or until golden brown. Cool on a wire rack.

Fragrant Swirl Loaf

Bread

1 cake yeast
2 cups warm (110° F.) milk
Approximately 6 cups unbleached
   all-purpose flour
1 tablespoon vegetable oil
4 teaspoons honey or sugar
3 eggs, at room temperature, lightly
   beaten
1/2 cup raisins
1/2 cup chopped nuts
Grated rind of 1 medium-size lemon
1 teaspoon salt

Filling

Melted butter
1 cup brown sugar
1 teaspoon cinnamon

Yield: 3 small loaves

In a 6-quart bowl, dissolve half the yeast in 1 cup milk. Add 1 cup flour. Mix well. Ferment in a warm (75° F.) place for 3 1/2 hours. Add the rest of the yeast and the milk. Mix well. Add the remaining bread ingredients, mixing the salt with the flour, and work into a dough. Turn onto a lightly floured surface and knead for 6 to 7 minutes, until smooth and elastic.

Return the dough to the mixing bowl and cover with a towel. Let rise in a warm (75° F.) place for 1 hour, or until doubled in bulk.

Divide the dough into 3 equal parts. Roll each piece into a rectangle 8 inches long by 6 inches wide and approximately 1 inch thick. Brush with melted butter. Combine the brown sugar and the cinnamon, and sprinkle it over the dough. Starting at the narrow end, roll each rectangle as you would a jelly roll. Set the loaves seam side down on a baking sheet that has been lightly greased with vegetable shortening. Cover the loaves with a towel and let them rise again for 50 minutes.

Bake in a preheated 350° F. oven for 45 minutes, or until golden brown. Cool on a wire rack.

Apple Streusel Bread

Bread

1 1/2 cakes yeast
2 cups warm (110° F.) milk
1 tablespoon vegetable oil
4 teaspoons honey or sugar
3 eggs, at room temperature, lightly beaten
2 apples, peeled and chopped
1/2 cup raisins
1/2 cup chopped nuts
Grated rind of 1 medium-size lemon
1 teaspoon salt
Approximately 6 cups unbleached all-purpose
  flour

Topping

1 egg, at room temperature, lightly beaten
1 tablespoon soft butter
1 tablespoon brown sugar
1/4 teaspoon cinnamon
4 teaspoons uncooked rolled oats

Yield: 3 small round loaves

In a 6-quart mixing bowl, dissolve the yeast in the milk. Add the remaining bread ingredients, mixing the salt with the remaining flour, and work them into a dough.

Turn the dough onto a lightly floured surface and knead it for 6 to 7 minutes, until the dough is smooth, elastic, and somewhat glossy.

Return the dough to the mixing bowl and cover with a towel. Let rise in a warm (75° F.) place for 1 hour, or until doubled in bulk.

Divide the dough into 3 equal parts and shape each piece into a round loaf. Flatten each loaf and set them on a baking sheet that has been lightly greased with vegetable shortening. Brush each loaf with the lightly beaten egg. Cream together the butter, the brown sugar, and the cinnamon. Add the oats. Mix well. Sprinkle this topping mixture over each loaf. Let the loaves rise again for 55 minutes.

Bake in a preheated 350° F. oven for 35 to 40 minutes, or until golden brown. Remove the loaves from the baking sheet at once and allow them to cool on a wire rack.

Royal Dutch Apple Loaf

Apples and cinnamon are just as Dutch as wooden shoes and dikes. This is a delicious loaf, especially good served warm with butter.

1 cake yeast
2 cups warm (110° F.) milk
Approximately 6 cups unbleached all-purpose
  flour
1 tablespoon vegetable oil
1 tablespoon honey or sugar
3 eggs, at room temperature, lightly beaten
2 apples, peeled and chopped
1/2 cup raisins
1/2 cup chopped walnuts
Grated rind of 1 lemon
Pinch cinnamon
Pinch mace
Pinch allspice
1 teaspoon salt

Yield: 2 medium-size round loaves

In a 6-quart mixing bowl, dissolve the yeast in the milk. Add 2 1/2 cups of the flour. Mix well. Let this ferment in a warm (75° F.) place for 30 minutes. Then add the remaining ingredients, mixing the salt with the remaining flour, and work them into a dough.

Turn the dough onto a lightly floured surface and knead it for 6 to 7 minutes, until the dough is smooth, elastic, and somewhat glossy.

Return the dough to the mixing bowl and cover with a towel. Let rise in a warm (75° F.) place for 1 hour, or until doubled in bulk.

Divide the dough into 2 equal halves and shape each piece into a round loaf. Set the loaves on a baking sheet that has been lightly greased with vegetable shortening. Cover the loaves with a towel and let them rise again for 50 minutes.

Bake in a preheated 350° F. oven for 50 minutes, or until golden brown. Remove the loaves from the baking sheet at once and allow them to cool on a wire rack.

Applesauce Loaf

This is a light bread with a spicy apple flavor—delicious for breakfast any morning.

1 cake yeast
1 1/2 cups warm (110° F.) skim milk
Approximately 6 cups unbleached all-purpose
  flour
3/4 cup applesauce, at room temperature
2 teaspoons vegetable oil
1 tablespoon honey or sugar
2 eggs, at room temperature, lightly beaten
Pinch mace
Pinch cinnamon
1 teaspoon salt

Yield: 2 medium-size loaves

In a 6-quart mixing bowl, dissolve half the yeast in 1 cup of the milk. Add 1 cup of the flour. Mix well. Let this ferment in a warm (75° F.) place for 3 1/2 hours. Then add the rest of the yeast and the milk. Mix well. Add the remaining ingredients, mixing the salt with the remaining flour, and work them into a dough.

Turn the dough onto a lightly floured surface and knead it for 6 to 7 minutes, until the dough is smooth, elastic, and somewhat glossy.

Return the dough to the mixing bowl and cover with a towel. Let rise in a warm (75° F.) place for 1 hour, or until doubled in bulk.

Divide the dough into 2 equal halves and shape each piece into an oblong loaf. Set on a baking sheet that has been lightly greased with vegetable shortening. Cover with a towel and let rise again for 55 minutes.

Bake in a preheated 350° F. oven for 50 minutes, or until golden brown. Remove from the baking sheet at once and cool on a wire rack.

Apricot Loaf

From Volendam, Holland.

Bread

1 cake yeast
1 3/4 cups warm (110° F.) skim milk
Approximately 6 cups unbleached all-purpose
    flour
1 tablespoon vegetable oil
4 teaspoons honey or sugar
3 eggs, at room temperature, lightly beaten
3/4 cup chopped dried apricots
1 tablespoon apricot jam or orange marmalade
Grated rind of 1 medium-size orange
1 teaspoon salt

Glaze

1 egg, at room temperature, lightly beaten
Sliced almonds

Yield: 2 medium-size round loaves

In a 6-quart mixing bowl, dissolve half the yeast in 1 cup milk. Add 1 cup flour. Mix well. Ferment in a warm (75° F.) place for 3 1/2 hours. Then add the rest of the yeast and the milk. Mix well. Add the remaining ingredients, mixing the salt with the remaining flour, and work them into a dough.

Turn the dough onto a lightly floured surface and knead it for 6 to 7 minutes, until the dough is smooth, elastic, and somewhat glossy.

Return the dough to the mixing bowl and cover with a towel. Let rise in a warm (75° F.) place for 1 hour, or until doubled in bulk.

Divide the dough into 2 equal halves and shape each into a round loaf. Set on a baking sheet that has been lightly greased with vegetable shortening. Cover with a towel and let rise again for 1 hour. Brush with the beaten egg and sprinkle with the sliced almonds.

Bake in a preheated 350° F. oven for 45 minutes, or until golden brown. Remove from the baking sheet and cool on a wire rack.

Apricot-Rum Bread

The Netherlands had many colonies around the world. From these faraway places came many exotic spices, liquors, and a variety of different foods, which found their way into the Dutch recipes. The inclusion of rum in this recipe is one of the many examples of this adaptation.

1 cake yeast
2 cups warm (110° F.) skim milk
Approximately 6 cups unbleached all-purpose
   flour
2 teaspoons vegetable oil
1 tablespoon sorghum or sugar
4 egg yolks, at room temperature
1 cup chopped dried apricots
Grated rind of 1 medium-size lemon
2 teaspoons rum
1/8 teaspoon pure vanilla extract
1 teaspoon salt

Yield: 2 medium-size loaves

In a 6-quart mixing bowl, dissolve the yeast in 1 cup of the milk. Add 1 cup of the flour. Mix well. Let this ferment in a warm (75° F.) place for 3 1/2 hours. Then add the rest of the yeast and the milk. Mix well. Add the remaining ingredients, mixing the salt with the remaining flour, and work them into a dough.

Turn the dough onto a lightly floured surface and knead it for 6 to 7 minutes, until the dough is smooth, elastic, and somewhat glossy.

Return the dough to the mixing bowl and cover with a towel. Let rise in a warm (75° F.) place for 1 hour, or until doubled in bulk.

Divide the dough into 2 equal halves and shape each piece into an oblong loaf. Set the loaves on a baking sheet that has been lightly greased with vegetable shortening. Cover the loaves with a towel and let them rise again for 50 to 55 minutes.

Bake in a preheated 350° F. oven for 50 minutes, or until golden brown. Remove from the baking sheet at once and cool on a wire rack.

Ginger Apricot Bread

This bread is especially good for breakfast with butter and honey.

1 cake yeast
2 cups warm (110° F.) milk
Approximately 6 cups unbleached all-purpose
 flour
2 teaspoons vegetable oil
1 tablespoon honey or sugar
2 eggs, at room temperature, lightly beaten
1/2 cup chopped dried apricots
Pinch ginger
1 teaspoon pure vanilla extract
1 teaspoon salt

Yield: 2 medium-size round loaves

In a 6-quart mixing bowl, dissolve half the yeast in 1 cup milk. Add 1 cup flour. Mix well. Ferment in a warm (75° F.) place for 3 1/2 hours. Then add the rest of the yeast and the milk. Mix well. Add the remaining ingredients, mixing the salt with the remaining flour, and work them into a dough.

Turn the dough onto a lightly floured surface and knead it for 6 to 7 minutes, until the dough is smooth, elastic, and somewhat glossy.

Return the dough to the mixing bowl and cover with a towel. Let rise in a warm (75° F.) place for 1 hour, or until doubled in bulk.

Divide the dough into 2 equal halves and shape each into a round loaf. Set on a baking sheet that has been lightly greased with vegetable shortening. Cover with a towel and let rise again for 50 minutes.

Bake in a preheated 375° F. oven for 40 minutes, or until golden brown. Remove the loaves from the baking sheet at once and allow them to cool on a wire rack.

Royal Fruit Bread

1/2 cup dried currants
1 cup raisins
1/2 cup brandy
1 cake yeast
2 cups warm (110° F.) milk
Approximately 6 cups unbleached all-purpose
   flour
2 teaspoons vegetable oil
4 teaspoons honey
3 eggs, at room temperature, lightly beaten
Grated rind of 1 lemon
Grated rind of 1 orange
Pinch cinnamon
Small pinch ginger
1 teaspoon salt

Yield: 2 medium-size loaves

Marinate the currants and the raisins in the brandy for 30 minutes.

In a 6-quart mixing bowl, dissolve half the yeast in 1 cup milk. Add 1 cup flour. Mix well. Ferment in a warm (75° F.) place for 3 1/2 hours. Then add the rest of the yeast and the milk. Mix well. Add the marinated currants and raisins and the remaining ingredients, mixing the salt with the remaining flour, and work them into a dough.

Turn the dough onto a lightly floured surface and knead it for 6 to 7 minutes, until the dough is smooth, elastic, and somewhat glossy.

Return the dough to the mixing bowl and cover with a towel. Let rise in a warm (75° F.) place for 1 hour, or until doubled in bulk.

Divide the dough into 2 equal halves and shape each into an oblong loaf. Set on a baking sheet that has been lightly greased with vegetable shortening. Cover and let rise again for 50 minutes.

Bake in a preheated 350° F. oven for 45 minutes, or until golden brown. Remove from the baking sheet and cool on a wire rack.

Portuguese Loaf

Portugal was at one time a strong maritime power, with many colonies throughout the world. Its old culture is rich and varied, and so is its food. Portugal produces good wine and, among its many agricultural products, an abundance of almonds. This recipe combines both these ingredients to make a delicious loaf.

1 cake yeast
2 cups warm (110° F.) skim milk
Approximately 6 cups unbleached all-purpose flour
4 teaspoons sweet wine
1/2 cup dried currants
1 tablespoon vegetable oil
1 tablespoon honey or sugar
4 egg yolks, at room temperature
1/2 cup chopped blanched almonds
Grated rind of 1 medium-size orange
Pinch saffron
1 teaspoon salt

Yield: 2 medium-size loaves

In a mixing bowl, dissolve half the yeast in 1 cup skim milk. Add 1 cup flour. Mix well. Ferment in a warm (75° F.) place for 3 1/2 hours. At the same time, mix the wine with the currants and marinate for 3 1/2 hours. To the fermented mixture, add the rest of the yeast and the milk. Mix well. Add the marinated currants and the remaining ingredients, mixing the salt with the remaining flour, and work into a dough.

Turn the dough onto a lightly floured surface and knead it for 6 to 7 minutes, until the dough is smooth, elastic, and somewhat glossy.

Return the dough to the mixing bowl and cover with a towel. Let rise in a warm (75° F.) place for 1 hour, or until doubled in bulk.

Divide the dough into 2 equal halves and shape each into an oblong loaf. Set the loaves on a baking sheet that has been lightly greased with vegetable shortening. Cover with a towel and let rise again for 50 minutes.

Bake in a preheated 375° F. oven for 45 minutes, or until golden brown. Remove from the baking sheet and cool on a wire rack.

Deluxe Raisin Bread

ᗢᗢ

This delightful raisin bread is moist – it will stay fresh for at least 3 days. It is very good toasted and served with cream cheese.

1 cake yeast
1 3/4 cups warm (110° F.) milk
Approximately 5 1/2 to 6 cups unbleached
   all-purpose flour
1 tablespoon vegetable oil
4 teaspoons honey or sugar
3 eggs, at room temperature, lightly beaten
1/2 cup grated carrots
1 cup raisins
1/2 cup chopped pecans
1 teaspoon salt

Yield: 2 medium-size loaves

In a 6-quart mixing bowl, dissolve half the yeast in 1 cup of the milk. Add 1 cup of the flour. Mix well. Let this ferment in a warm (75° F.) place for 3 1/2 hours. Then add the rest of the yeast and the milk. Mix well. Add the remaining ingredients, mixing the salt with the remaining flour, and work them into a dough.

Turn the dough onto a lightly floured surface and knead it for 6 to 7 minutes, until the dough is smooth, elastic, and somewhat glossy.

Return the dough to the mixing bowl and cover with a towel. Let rise in a warm (75° F.) place for 1 hour, or until doubled in bulk.

Divide the dough into 2 equal halves and shape each into an oblong loaf. Set on a baking sheet that has been lightly greased with vegetable shortening. Cover with a towel and let rise again for 50 minutes.

Bake in a preheated 350° F. oven for 50 minutes, or until golden brown. Remove the loaves from the baking sheet at once and allow them to cool on a wire rack.

German Stollen

Stollen is a sweet bread that originated in Germany, where it was baked mainly for festive or special occasions. There are many variations of it, all equally delicious.

1 cake yeast
2 cups warm (110° F.) milk
Approximately 6 cups unbleached all-purpose
    flour
1 tablespoon vegetable oil
1 tablespoon honey or sugar
2 eggs, at room temperature, lightly beaten
1/2 cup chopped candied fruit
1/2 cup raisins
1/2 cup chopped nuts
Grated rind of 1 medium-size lemon
1 teaspoon salt

Yield: 1 large loaf

In a 6-quart mixing bowl, dissolve the yeast in the milk. Add 2 1/2 cups of the flour. Mix well. Let this ferment in a warm (75° F.) place for 30 minutes. Add the remaining ingredients, mixing the salt with the remaining flour, and work them into a dough.

Turn the dough onto a lightly floured surface and knead it for 6 to 7 minutes, until the dough is smooth, elastic, and somewhat glossy.

Return the dough to the mixing bowl and cover it with a towel. Let the dough rise in a warm (75° F.) place for 1 hour, or until doubled in bulk.

Shape the dough into an oblong loaf. Set the loaf on a lightly greased baking sheet. Cover it with a towel and let it rise again for 50 minutes.

Bake in a preheated 350° F. oven for 55 minutes, or until golden brown. Remove the loaf from the baking sheet at once and allow it to cool on a wire rack.

Rhineland Stollen

∞∞∞

In Germany there are as many stollen recipes as there are bakeries. This particular recipe originated in Rhineland around Adenau.

1 cake yeast
1 3/4 cups warm (110° F.) milk
Approximately 6 cups unbleached all-purpose
 flour
1 tablespoon vegetable oil
1 tablespoon honey or sugar
4 eggs, at room temperature, lightly beaten
1/2 cup raisins
1/4 cup chopped citron
1/2 cup chopped nuts
Grated rind of 1 medium-size orange
Grated rind of 1 medium-size lemon
Pinch nutmeg
1 teaspoon salt

Yield: 2 medium-size loaves

In a 6-quart mixing bowl, dissolve half the yeast in 1 cup milk. Add 1 cup flour. Mix well. Ferment in a warm (75° F.) place for 3 1/2 hours. Then add the rest of the yeast and the milk. Mix well. Add the remaining ingredients, mixing the salt with the remaining flour, and work into a dough.

Turn the dough onto a lightly floured surface and knead it for 6 to 7 minutes, until the dough is smooth, elastic, and somewhat glossy.

Return the dough to the mixing bowl and cover with a towel. Let rise in a warm (75° F.) place for 1 hour, or until doubled in bulk.

Divide the dough into 2 equal halves and shape each into an oblong loaf. Set on a baking sheet that has been lightly greased with vegetable shortening. Cover with a towel and let rise again for 50 minutes.

Bake in a preheated 350° F. oven for 50 minutes, or until golden brown. Remove the loaves from the baking sheet at once and allow them to cool on a wire rack.

Royal Dutch Spiced Bread

At my grandfather's bakery, we had many sweet breads in our repertoire, but we baked only a few types each weekend. This one had a lot of customers waiting for it.

1 cake yeast
1 1/2 cups warm (110° F.) milk
Approximately 5 1/2 to 6 cups unbleached
   all-purpose flour
2 teaspoons vegetable oil
4 teaspoons honey or sugar
2 eggs, at room temperature, lightly beaten
1/2 cup raisins
Grated rind of 1 medium-size lemon
Grated rind of 1 medium-size orange
1/2 cup rum
Pinch cinnamon
Pinch ginger
1 teaspoon salt

Yield: 2 medium-size loaves

In a 6-quart mixing bowl, dissolve half the yeast in the milk. Add 1 cup of the flour. Mix well. Let this ferment in a warm (75° F.) place for 3 1/2 hours. Then add the rest of the yeast and the milk. Mix well. Add the remaining ingredients, mixing the salt with the remaining flour, and work them into a dough.

Turn the dough onto a lightly floured surface and knead it for 6 to 7 minutes, until the dough is smooth, elastic, and somewhat glossy.

Return the dough to the mixing bowl and cover with a towel. Let rise in a warm (75° F.) place for 1 hour, or until doubled in bulk.

Divide the dough into 2 equal halves and shape each piece into an oblong loaf. Set the loaves on a baking sheet that has been lightly greased with vegetable shortening. Cover the loaves with a towel and let them rise again for 50 minutes.

Bake in a preheated 375° F. oven for 35 to 40 minutes, or until golden brown. Remove from the baking sheet at once and cool on a wire rack.

Spiced Dutch Ginger Bread

This is a traditional bread from the coastal area around Den Helder in North Holland. This bread is especially good on a wintry day with Dutch coffee (half coffee, half chocolate).

1 cake yeast
2 cups warm (110° F.) milk
Approximately 6 cups unbleached all-purpose
  flour
2 teaspoons vegetable oil
4 teaspoons honey or sugar
2 eggs, at room temperature, lightly beaten
1/4 cup chopped candied orange peel
Pinch ginger
Pinch cloves
Pinch cinnamon
Pinch mace
1 teaspoon salt

Yield: 2 medium-size round loaves

In a 6-quart mixing bowl, dissolve half the yeast in 1 cup of the milk. Add 1 cup of the flour. Mix well. Let this ferment in a warm (75° F.) place for 3 1/2 hours. Then add the rest of the yeast and the milk. Mix well. Add the remaining ingredients, mixing the salt with the remaining flour, and work them into a dough.

Turn the dough onto a lightly floured surface and knead it for 6 to 7 minutes, until the dough is smooth, elastic, and somewhat glossy.

Return the dough to the mixing bowl and cover with a towel. Let rise in a warm (75° F.) place for 1 hour, or until doubled in bulk.

Divide the dough into 2 equal halves and shape each into a round loaf. Set on a baking sheet that has been lightly greased with vegetable shortening. Cover and let rise again for 1 hour.

Bake in a preheated 375° F. oven for 40 minutes, or until golden brown. Remove the loaves from the baking sheet at once and allow them to cool on a wire rack.

Original Deluxe Bread

This is one of my own favorite recipes. It makes a moist, sweet, and rich-tasting bread that will keep fresh for several days. It is very good with a mild cheese.

1 cake yeast
1 3/4 cups warm (110° F.) milk
Approximately 5 1/2 to 6 cups unbleached
   all-purpose flour
4 teaspoons vegetable oil
4 teaspoons honey or sugar
4 eggs, at room temperature, lightly beaten
Grated rind of 1 medium-size orange
2 teaspoons light rum
Pinch mace
1 teaspoon salt

Yield: 2 medium-size round loaves

In a 6-quart mixing bowl, dissolve half the yeast in 1 cup of the milk. Add 1 cup of the flour. Mix well. Let this ferment in a warm (75° F.) place for 3 1/2 hours. Then add the rest of the yeast and the milk. Mix well. Add the remaining ingredients, mixing the salt with the remaining flour, and work them into a dough.

Turn the dough onto a lightly floured surface and knead it for 6 to 7 minutes, until the dough is smooth, elastic, and somewhat glossy.

Return the dough to the mixing bowl and cover with a towel. Let rise in a warm (75° F.) place for 1 hour, or until doubled in bulk.

Divide the dough into 2 equal halves and shape each into a round loaf. Set on a baking sheet that has been lightly greased with vegetable shortening. Cover with a towel and let rise again for 50 minutes.

Bake in a preheated 350° F. oven for 50 minutes, or until golden brown. Remove from the baking sheet at once and cool on a wire rack.

Sweet Almond Bread

∞∞

*Another weekend bread that you can bake any day.
It is a loaf with a sweet almond flavor and a fine
texture.*

1 cake yeast
2 cups warm (110° F.) milk
Approximately 6 cups unbleached all-purpose
   flour
2 teaspoons vegetable oil
1/4 cup honey or sugar
2 eggs, at room temperature, lightly beaten
1/2 cup chopped almonds
1 teaspoon pure almond extract
1 teaspoon salt

Yield: 2 medium-size loaves

In a 6-quart mixing bowl, dissolve half the yeast in 1 cup of the milk. Add 1 cup of the flour. Mix well. Let this ferment in a warm (75° F.) place for 3 1/2 hours. Then add the rest of the yeast and the milk. Mix well. Add the remaining ingredients, mixing the salt with the remaining flour, and work them into a dough.

Turn the dough onto a lightly floured surface and knead it for 6 to 7 minutes, until the dough is smooth, elastic, and somewhat glossy.

Return the dough to the mixing bowl and cover with a towel. Let rise in a warm (75° F.) place for 1 hour, or until doubled in bulk.

Divide the dough into 2 equal halves and shape each into an oblong loaf. Set on a baking sheet that has been lightly greased with vegetable shortening. Cover with a towel and let rise again for 1 hour.

Bake in a preheated 375° F. oven for 40 minutes, or until golden brown. Remove from the baking sheet at once and cool on a wire rack.

Belgian Pecan Loaf

Sunday afternoons or early evenings many European families enjoy a leisurely meal together before the beginning of another work week. They serve a sweet bread like this one with butter and jam and other sweets, and end their meal with fruit and cheese.

1 cake yeast
2 cups warm (110° F.) skim milk
Approximately 6 cups unbleached all-purpose flour
2 teaspoons vegetable oil
1 tablespoon sorghum or sugar
4 egg yolks, at room temperature
1 cup chopped pecans
Pinch mace
Pinch cinnamon
1 teaspoon salt

Yield: 2 medium-size round loaves

In a 6-quart mixing bowl, dissolve half the yeast in 1 cup of the milk. Add 1 cup of the flour. Mix well. Let this ferment in a warm (75° F.) place for 3 1/2 hours. Then add the rest of the yeast and the milk. Mix well. Add the remaining ingredients, mixing the salt with the remaining flour, and work them into a dough.

Turn the dough onto a lightly floured surface and knead it for 6 to 7 minutes, until the dough is smooth, elastic, and somewhat glossy.

Return the dough to the mixing bowl and cover with a towel. Let rise in a warm (75° F.) place for 1 hour, or until doubled in bulk.

Divide the dough into 2 equal halves and shape each into a round loaf. Set on a baking sheet that has been lightly greased with vegetable shortening. Cover with a towel and let rise again for 50 minutes.

Bake in a preheated 350° F. oven for 45 to 50 minutes, or until golden brown. Remove from the baking sheet at once and cool on a wire rack.

Royal Castilian Loaf

In the region of Castile, north of Madrid, the shepherds have their own cuisine. Though the plains are mostly arid, many areas do produce wheat. Bread is often baked in wood-fired ovens. This loaf is very good with butter and jam.

1 cake yeast
2 cups warm (110° F.) skim milk
Approximately 6 cups unbleached all-purpose flour
1 tablespoon vegetable oil
1 tablespoon honey or sugar
4 egg yolks, at room temperature
1/2 cup dried currants
1/2 cup chopped roasted unsalted peanuts
Pinch powdered saffron
1 teaspoon salt

Yield: 2 medium-size loaves

In a 6-quart mixing bowl, dissolve half the yeast in 1 cup milk. Add 1 cup flour. Mix well. Ferment in a warm (75° F.) place for 3 1/2 hours. Then add the rest of the yeast and the milk. Mix well. Add the remaining ingredients, mixing the salt with the remaining flour, and work them into a dough.

Turn the dough onto a lightly floured surface and knead it for 6 to 7 minutes, until the dough is smooth, elastic, and somewhat glossy.

Return the dough to the mixing bowl and cover with a towel. Let rise in a warm (75° F.) place for 1 hour, or until doubled in bulk.

Divide the dough into 2 equal halves and shape each into an oblong loaf. Set on a baking sheet that has been lightly greased with vegetable shortening. Cover with a towel and let rise again for 50 minutes.

Bake in a preheated 350° F. oven for 50 minutes, or until golden brown. Remove the loaves from the baking sheet at once and allow them to cool on a wire rack.

Rum Honey Bread

oooooooooooooooooooooooooooooooooooooooooooooooooooooooooooooooooooo

This delightful lemony bread originated during the Dutch colonial times. Rum was imported from Surinam, and the addition of it in this bread gave it an exquisite taste.

1 cake yeast
2 cups warm (110° F.) milk
Approximately 6 cups unbleached all-purpose
  flour
2 teaspoons vegetable oil
4 teaspoons honey or sugar
2 eggs, at room temperature, lightly beaten
Grated rind of 1 medium-size lemon
1/4 cup light rum
1 teaspoon salt

Yield: 2 medium-size loaves

In a 6-quart mixing bowl, dissolve half the yeast in 1 cup milk. Add 1 cup flour. Mix well. Ferment in a warm (75° F.) place for 3 1/2 hours. Then add the rest of the yeast and the milk. Mix well. Add the remaining ingredients, mixing the salt with the remaining flour, and work them into a dough.

Turn the dough onto a lightly floured surface and knead it for 6 to 7 minutes, until the dough is smooth, elastic, and somewhat glossy.

Return the dough to the mixing bowl and cover with a towel. Let rise in a warm (75° F.) place for 1 hour, or until doubled in bulk.

Divide the dough into 2 equal halves and shape each into an oblong loaf. Set on a baking sheet that has been lightly greased with vegetable shortening. Cover with a towel and let rise again for 50 minutes.

Bake in a preheated 375° F. oven for 40 minutes, or until golden brown. Remove the loaves from the baking sheet at once and allow them to cool on a wire rack.

Golden Carrot Bread

This bread, which I used to bake in Holland, was entered in the Wyoming State Fair and won first prize in 1972. It will keep well in a bread box.

1 cake yeast
2 cups warm (110° F.) milk
Approximately 6 cups unbleached all-purpose
    flour
2 teaspoons vegetable oil
1 tablespoon honey or sugar
2 eggs, at room temperature, lightly beaten
1/2 cup grated carrots
1 teaspoon salt

Yield: 2 medium-size round loaves

In a 6-quart mixing bowl, dissolve half the yeast in 1 cup milk. Add 1 cup flour. Mix well. Ferment in a warm (75° F.) place for 3 1/2 hours. Then add the rest of the yeast and the milk. Mix well. Add the remaining ingredients, mixing the salt with the remaining flour, and work them into a dough.

Turn the dough onto a lightly floured surface and knead it for 6 to 7 minutes, until the dough is smooth, elastic, and somewhat glossy.

Return the dough to the mixing bowl and cover with a towel. Let rise in a warm (75° F.) place for 1 hour, or until doubled in bulk.

Divide the dough into 2 equal halves and shape each into a round loaf. Set on a baking sheet that has been lightly greased with vegetable shortening. Cover with a towel and let rise again for 50 minutes.

Bake in a preheated 350° F. oven for 50 minutes, or until golden brown. Remove the loaves from the baking sheet at once and allow them to cool on a wire rack.

Fruit Tulband

Originally the Dutch word band *was* tulband, *which came from the word turban, a headdress worn in the Middle East. Over the centuries it became* tulban *and then* band. *This word was used to describe bread baked in a fluted tube pan. The German counterpart is called* bundt *or* Gugelhupf.

1 cake yeast
2 cups warm (110° F.) skim milk
Approximately 6 cups unbleached all-purpose
   flour
2 teaspoons vegetable oil
4 teaspoons honey or sugar
2 eggs, at room temperature, lightly beaten
1 cup chopped candied fruit
1 cup raisins
Grated rind of 1 medium-size lemon
Pinch mace
1 teaspoon salt
Powdered sugar

Yield: 1 large loaf

In a 6-quart mixing bowl, dissolve half the yeast in 1 cup of the milk. Add 1 cup of the flour. Mix well. Let this ferment in a warm (75° F.) place for 3 1/2 hours. Then add the rest of the yeast and the milk. Mix well. Add the remaining ingredients, except the powdered sugar, mixing the salt with the remaining flour, and work them into a dough.

Turn the dough onto a lightly floured surface and knead it for 6 to 7 minutes, until the dough is smooth, elastic, and somewhat glossy.

Return the dough to the mixing bowl and cover with a towel. Let rise in a warm (75° F.) place for 1 hour, or until doubled in bulk.

Shape the dough into a round loaf with a hole in the middle. Set the loaf into a well-greased tube or bundt pan. Cover it with a towel and let it rise again for 55 minutes.

Bake in a preheated 375° F. oven for 50 minutes, or until golden brown. Remove from the baking pan and cool on a wire rack. Dust with powdered sugar while still warm.

Dutch Tulband Loaf

In the Dutch part of Flanders, the bundt loaf is usually reserved for special occasions, such as weddings or wedding anniversaries.

1 cake yeast
1 1/2 cups warm (110° F.) skim milk
Approximately 6 cups unbleached all-purpose
    flour
4 teaspoons vegetable oil
7 teaspoons honey or sugar
2 eggs, at room temperature, lightly beaten
2 egg yolks, at room temperature
1 cup raisins
1 cup chopped dates
1/2 cup chopped pecans
Grated rind of 1 medium-size lemon
Pinch nutmeg
Pinch cinnamon
1 teaspoon salt
Powdered sugar

Yield: 1 large loaf

In a 6-quart mixing bowl, dissolve half the yeast in 1 cup of the milk. Add 1 cup of the flour. Mix well. Let this ferment in a warm (75° F.) place for 3 1/2 hours. Then add the rest of the yeast and the milk. Mix well. Add the remaining ingredients, except the powdered sugar, mixing the salt with the remaining flour, and work them into a dough.

Turn the dough onto a lightly floured surface and knead it for 6 to 7 minutes, until the dough is smooth, elastic, and somewhat glossy.

Return the dough to the mixing bowl and cover with a towel. Let rise in a warm (75° F.) place for 1 hour, or until doubled in bulk.

Shape the dough into a round loaf with a hole in the middle. Set the loaf in a well-greased tube or bundt pan. Cover it with a towel and let it rise again for 1 hour.

Bake in a preheated 350° F. oven for 50 to 55 minutes, or until golden brown. Remove from the baking pan and cool on a wire rack. Dust with powdered sugar while still warm.

Wedding Tulband

Bread

1 cake yeast
2 cups warm (110° F.) milk
Approximately 6 cups unbleached all-purpose
  flour
1 tablespoon vegetable oil
4 teaspoons honey or sugar
4 egg yolks, at room temperature
1/4 cup dried currants
1/2 cup raisins
1/2 cup candied fruit
1/4 cup chopped pecans
Grated rind of 1 medium-size lemon
1 teaspoon salt

Glaze

1 egg white, at room temperature, lightly beaten
Sliced almonds

Yield: 1 big loaf

In a 6-quart bowl, dissolve half the yeast in 1 cup milk. Add 1 cup flour. Mix well. Ferment in a warm (75° F.) place for 3 1/2 hours. Then add the rest of the yeast and the milk. Mix well. Add the remaining bread ingredients, mixing the salt with the flour, and work into a dough.

Turn the dough onto a lightly floured surface and knead it for 6 to 7 minutes, until the dough is smooth, elastic, and somewhat glossy.

Return the dough to the mixing bowl and cover with a towel. Let rise in a warm (75° F.) place for 1 hour, or until doubled in bulk.

Shape the dough into a round loaf with a hole in the middle. Set in a tube or bundt pan that has been well greased with vegetable shortening. Brush with the egg white and sprinkle with the almonds. Cover and let rise again for 1 hour.

Bake in a preheated 375° F. oven for 50 minutes, or until golden brown. Remove from the baking pan and cool on a wire rack.

Saffron Bundt Loaf

This is another festive loaf for a special occasion. An angel food cake pan can be used instead of a bundt pan.

1 cake yeast
1 cup warm (110° F.) skim milk
Approximately 6 cups unbleached all-purpose flour
Small pinch saffron
1 cup very hot water
1 tablespoon vegetable oil
4 teaspoons honey or sugar
3 eggs, at room temperature, lightly beaten
Grated rind of 1 medium-size orange
1 teaspoon salt

Yield: 1 large loaf

In a 6-quart mixing bowl, dissolve half the yeast in 1 cup of the milk. Add 1 cup of the flour. Mix well. Let this ferment in a warm (75° F.) place for 3 1/2 hours. Meanwhile, mix the saffron in the very hot water and let it stand at room temperature for 3 1/2 hours. Then add the saffron tea and the rest of the yeast to the fermented mixture. Mix well. Add the remaining ingredients, mixing the salt with the remaining flour, and work them into a dough.

Turn the dough onto a lightly floured surface and knead it for 6 to 7 minutes, until the dough is smooth, elastic, and somewhat glossy.

Return the dough to the mixing bowl and cover with a towel. Let rise in a warm (75° F.) place for 1 hour, or until doubled in bulk.

Shape the dough into a round loaf with a hole in the middle. Set into a well-greased bundt pan. Cover with a towel and let rise again for 1 hour.

Bake in a preheated 375° F. oven for 50 minutes, or until golden brown. Remove from the baking pan and cool on a wire rack.

Jewish Onion Bread

∞∞∞

This was a very popular bread in the Jordan district of Amsterdam before World War II. It is a nice accompaniment to vegetable soup.

Bread

1 cake yeast
2 cups warm (110° F.) potato cooking water
1 egg, at room temperature, lightly beaten
2 teaspoons vegetable oil
1 medium-size onion, finely chopped
1 teaspoon salt
Approximately 6 cups unbleached all-purpose
  flour

Glaze

1 egg, at room temperature, lightly beaten
Sesame seeds

Yield: 2 medium-size loaves

In a 6-quart mixing bowl, dissolve the yeast in the potato cooking water. Add the remaining ingredients, mixing the salt with the remaining flour, and work them into a dough.

Turn the dough onto a lightly floured surface and knead it for 6 to 7 minutes, until the dough is smooth, elastic, and somewhat glossy.

Return the dough to the mixing bowl and cover it with a towel. Let the dough rise in a warm (75° F.) place for 1 hour, or until doubled in bulk.

Divide the dough into 2 equal halves and shape each piece into an oblong loaf. Set the loaves on a baking sheet that has been lightly greased with vegetable shortening. Cover the loaves with a towel and let them rise again for 50 minutes. Brush the loaves lightly with the beaten egg and sprinkle with the sesame seeds.

Bake in a preheated 375° F. oven for 45 minutes, or until golden brown. Remove the loaves from the baking sheet at once and allow them to cool on a wire rack.

Bacon and Cheese Bread

This is a very old Dutch recipe. The bread is delicious with Edam cheese and dark Dutch beer.

1 cake yeast
2 cups warm (110° F.) milk
Approximately 6 cups unbleached all-purpose
   flour
1 teaspoon vegetable oil
1 egg, at room temperature, lightly beaten
1/2 cup grated cheddar cheese
1/2 cup fried crisp bacon bits
1 teaspoon salt

Yield: 2 medium-size loaves

In a 6-quart mixing bowl, dissolve half the yeast in 1 cup of the milk. Add 1 cup of the flour. Mix well. Let this ferment in a warm (75° F.) place for 3 1/2 hours. Then add the rest of the yeast and the milk. Mix well. Add the remaining ingredients, mixing the salt with the remaining flour, and work them into a dough.

Turn the dough onto a lightly floured surface and knead it for 6 to 7 minutes, until the dough is smooth, elastic, and somewhat glossy.

Return the dough to the mixing bowl and cover with a towel. Let rise in a warm (75° F.) place for 1 hour, or until doubled in bulk.

Divide the dough into 2 equal halves and shape each into an oblong loaf. Set on a lightly greased baking sheet. Cover and let rise again for 50 minutes.

Bake in a preheated 375° F. oven for 40 minutes, or until golden brown. Remove the loaves from the baking sheet at once and allow them to cool on a wire rack.

Bohemian-Style Cheese Bread

This bread comes from the Bohemian forest region between Germany and Czechoslovakia. It is delicious, especially when served with cold cuts and beer.

1 1/2 cakes yeast (or 4 1/2 teaspoons dry yeast)
2 cups warm (110° F.) water
2 1/4 cups rye flour
1 teaspoon sorghum or sugar
1 cup grated cheddar cheese
1 teaspoon caraway seeds
1 teaspoon salt
Approximately 4 cups unbleached all-purpose
    flour

Yield: 2 medium-size round loaves

In a 1/2 quart jar, dissolve 1/2 cake yeast (or 1 1/2 teaspoons dry yeast) in a 1/4 cup of the water. Add 1/4 cup of the rye flour. Mix well. Let this ferment overnight in a warm (75° F.) place.

The next morning, place the fermented mixture in a 6-quart mixing bowl, and add the remaining 1 cake yeast (or 3 teaspoons dry yeast), 1 cup warm water, and 1 cup of the rye flour. Mix well and let this ferment in a warm place for 2 1/2 hours. Then, add the remaining 1 cup of rye flour, 3/4 cup warm water and all the remaining ingredients, mixing the salt with the remaining flour, and work them into a dough.

Turn the dough onto a lightly floured surface and knead it for 6 to 7 minutes, until the dough is smooth, elastic, and somewhat glossy.

Return the dough to the mixing bowl and cover it with a towel. Let the dough rise in a warm (75° F.) place for 1 hour, or until doubled in bulk.

Divide the dough into 2 equal halves and shape each piece into a round loaf and set them on a lightly floured surface. Cover the loaves with a towel and let them rise for 15 minutes. Reshape each loaf again into a round loaf to work out the air. Set the loaves on a baking sheet that has been liberally dusted with corn meal. Cover the loaves with a towel and let them rise again for 40 minutes.

Bake in a preheated 375° F. oven for 45 minutes, or until golden brown. Remove the loaves from the baking sheet at once and allow them to cool on a wire rack.

Greek Cheese Bread

This bread is perfect for entertaining. All you need with it is a little whipped butter and a glass of wine.

1 cake yeast
2 cups warm (110° F.) water
Approximately 6 1/4 cups unbleached
   all-purpose flour
8 ounces feta cheese, at room temperature
2 teaspoons honey or sugar
3 eggs, at room temperature
1 teaspoon salt

Yield: 2 large round loaves

In a 6-quart mixing bowl, dissolve half the yeast into 1 cup water. Add 1 cup flour. Mix well. Ferment for 3 hours in a warm (75° F.) place.

In a 1-quart mixing bowl, crumble the feta cheese. Add the honey, eggs, and salt. Mix well. Keep this in a warm place.

To the mixture in the big (6-quart) bowl, add the rest of the yeast and the water. Mix well. Then add the cheese mixture and the remaining 5 1/4 cups flour, working this into a dough.

Turn the dough onto a lightly floured surface and knead for 6 to 7 minutes, until the dough is smooth, elastic, and somewhat glossy.

Return the dough to the mixing bowl and cover with a towel. Let rise in a warm (75° F.) place for 1 hour, or until doubled in bulk.

Divide the dough into 2 equal halves and shape each into a round loaf. Set on a lightly greased baking sheet. Cover with a towel and let rise again for 50 minutes.

Bake in a preheated 350° F. oven for 50 minutes, or until golden brown. Cool on a wire rack.

Der Hungry Dutchman Bread

This is one of my original recipes for a light bread. It makes good sandwiches, and it goes especially well with Gouda cheese.

1 cake yeast
2 cups warm (110° F.) milk
Approximately 5 cups unbleached all-purpose flour
1 teaspoon vegetable oil
1 egg, at room temperature, lightly beaten
1/2 cup grated cheese
1 teaspoon salt
1 cup whole wheat flour

Yield: 2 medium-size loaves

In a 6-quart mixing bowl, dissolve half the yeast in 1 cup of the milk. Add 1 cup of the all-purpose flour. Mix well. Let this ferment in a warm (75° F.) place for 3 1/2 hours. Then add the rest of the yeast and the milk. Mix well. Add the remaining ingredients, mixing the salt in with the remaining flours, and work them into a dough.

Turn the dough onto a lightly floured surface and knead for 6 to 7 minutes, until the dough is smooth, elastic, and somewhat glossy.

Return the dough to the mixing bowl and cover with a towel. Let rise in a warm (75° F.) place for 1 hour, or until doubled in bulk.

Divide the dough into 2 equal halves and shape each into an oblong loaf. Set on a baking sheet that has been lightly greased with vegetable shortening. Cover with a towel and let rise again for 50 minutes.

Bake in a preheated 375° F. oven for 40 minutes, or until golden brown. Remove from the baking sheet and cool on a wire rack.

Milano Corn Bread

Italy, the land of pasta, has a great variety of different breads. Here's a corn bread with a difference.

1 cake yeast
2 cups warm (110° F.) milk
2 teaspoons vegetable oil
1 tablespoon honey or sugar
2 eggs, at room temperature, lightly beaten
1/2 cup chopped nuts
1/2 cup cornmeal
1 teaspoon salt
Approximately 5 1/2 cups unbleached
 all-purpose flour

Yield: 2 medium-size loaves

In a 6-quart mixing bowl, dissolve the yeast in the milk. Add the remaining ingredients, mixing the salt with the remaining flour, and work them into a dough.

Turn the dough onto a lightly floured surface and knead it for 6 to 7 minutes, until the dough is smooth, elastic, and somewhat glossy.

Return the dough to the mixing bowl and cover it with a towel. Let the dough rise in a warm (75° F.) place for 1 hour, or until doubled in bulk.

Divide the dough into 2 equal halves and shape each piece into an oblong loaf. Set the loaves on a baking sheet that has been lightly greased with vegetable shortening. Cover the loaves with a towel and let them rise again for 50 minutes.

Bake in a preheated 375° F. oven for 40 minutes, or until golden brown. Remove the loaves from the baking sheet at once and allow them to cool on a wire rack.

Dutch Beer Bread

The baking of bread and the brewing of beer both date from antiquity, but the combining of both into one is really Dutch.

1 cake yeast
1 cup warm (110° F.) water
1 cup whole wheat flour
1 cup warm (110° F.) beer
2 teaspoons vegetable oil
2 teaspoons honey or sugar
1 egg, at room temperature, lightly beaten
1 teaspoon salt
Approximately 5 cups unbleached all-purpose
   flour

Yield: 2 medium-size round loaves

In a 6-quart mixing bowl, dissolve half the yeast in the water. Add the whole wheat flour. Mix well. Ferment in a warm (75° F.) place for 3 1/2 hours. Then add the rest of the yeast and the beer. Mix well. Add the remaining ingredients, mixing the salt in with the remaining flour, and work into a dough.

Turn the dough onto a lightly floured surface and knead for 6 to 7 minutes, until the dough is smooth, elastic, and somewhat glossy.

Return the dough to the mixing bowl and cover with a towel. Let rise in a warm (75° F.) place for 50 minutes, or until doubled in bulk.

Divide the dough into 2 equal halves and shape each into a round loaf. Set on a baking sheet that has been liberally dusted with cornmeal. Cover with a towel and let rise again for 45 to 50 minutes.

Bake in a preheated 375° F. oven for 45 minutes, or until golden brown. Remove the loaves from the baking sheet at once and allow them to cool on a wire rack.

Italian Olive Bread

That's Italian: a big platter of this bread with plenty of salami, prosciutto, provolone cheese, and a glass of good Italian wine. Finish with a cup of expresso.

1 cake yeast
2 cups warm (110° F.) water
1 teaspoon honey
Approximately 6 1/4 cups unbleached
   all-purpose flour
1 tablespoon vegetable oil
3 eggs, at room temperature, lightly beaten
5 ounces pimiento stuffed olives, drained and
   chopped (about 1 cup)
3 ounces cream cheese
Pinch chopped chives
1 teaspoon salt

Yield: 2 medium-size loaves

In a 6-quart mixing bowl, dissolve half the yeast in 1 cup of the water. Add the honey and 1 cup of the flour. Mix well. Let this ferment in a warm (75° F.) place for 3 1/2 hours. Then add the rest of the yeast and the water. Mix well. Add the remaining ingredients, mixing the salt in with the remaining flour, and work them into a dough.

Turn the dough onto a lightly floured surface and knead for 6 to 7 minutes, until the dough is smooth, elastic, and somewhat glossy.

Return the dough to the mixing bowl and cover with a towel. Let rise in a warm (75° F.) place for 50 to 60 minutes, or until doubled in bulk.

Divide the dough into 2 equal halves and shape each into an oblong loaf. Set on a lightly greased baking sheet. Cover and let rise again for 50 minutes.

Bake in a preheated 350° F. oven for 50 minutes, or until golden brown. Remove from the baking sheet at once and cool on a wire rack.

Ella's Lenzen Brot

∞∞

Most bakers experiment with their recipes. Ella, my mother-in-law, loved lentils, so this recipe was created in her memory. This is a good bread for sandwiches.

1/4 cup dried lentils
2 cups warm (110° F.) water
1 cake yeast
1 teaspoon vegetable oil
2 teaspoons honey or sugar
1 egg, at room temperature, lightly beaten
1 teaspoon salt
Approximately 5 1/2 cups unbleached
   all-purpose flour

Yield: 2 medium-size loaves

In a 6-quart mixing bowl, place the lentils in 1 cup of the water. Let this soak overnight in a warm (75° F.) place. The next day add the remaining 1 cup warm water and dissolve the yeast in this mixture. Add the remaining ingredients, mixing the salt in with the flour, and work them into a dough.

Turn the dough onto a lightly floured surface and knead for 6 to 7 minutes, until the dough is smooth, elastic, and somewhat glossy.

Return the dough to the mixing bowl and cover with a towel. Let rise in a warm (75° F.) place for 1 hour, or until doubled in bulk.

Divide the dough into 2 equal halves and shape each piece into an oblong loaf. Set on a baking sheet that has been lightly greased with vegetable shortening. Cover with a towel and let rise again for 50 minutes.

Bake in a preheated 375° F. oven for 50 minutes, or until golden brown. Remove from the baking sheet and cool on a wire rack, wrapped in a towel so the lentils on the outside of the bread stay soft.

Ingrid's Pizza Dough

Most pizza dough recipes come from Italy. This one took the scenic route through Brazil, and now finds its home in Wyoming.

1 cake yeast
1 cup warm (110° F.) water
4 teaspoons olive oil
3/4 teaspoon salt
Approximately 2 1/2 cups unbleached
   all-purpose flour

Yield: 1 large pizza

In a 6-quart mixing bowl, dissolve the yeast in the water. Add the remaining ingredients, working them into a dough.

Turn the dough onto a lightly floured surface and knead for 6 to 7 minutes, until the dough is smooth, elastic, and somewhat glossy.

Return the dough to the mixing bowl and cover it with a towel. Let rise in a warm (75° F.) place for 45 minutes, or until doubled in bulk.

With a rolling pin, roll out the dough to the size of your pizza pie pan. Set into a pizza pie pan that has been lightly greased with olive oil. Spread tomato sauce over the dough and sprinkle your favorite topping over it. In Brazil, in place of tomato sauce, they cover the dough with thin slices of fresh tomato and then cover these with cheese and different kind of toppings. One of Ingrid's favorite toppings there is chopped escarole. Sprinkle with grated mozzarella cheese, Parmesan cheese, oregano, and a few drops of olive oil. Let the dough rise for 20 minutes.

Bake in a preheated 400° F. oven for 15 to 20 minutes.

Stuffing Bread

This is an excellent bread to use to make stuffing for roast goose or chicken.

1/2 cake yeast
1 cup warm (110° F.) water
1 egg, at room temperature, lightly beaten
1 teaspoon finely chopped parsley
1 teaspoon chopped celery leaves
1/2 teaspoon finely chopped onion
Pinch thyme
Pinch sage
Pinch marjoram
3/4 cup cornmeal
1/2 teaspoon salt
Approximately 2 cups unbleached all-purpose
   flour

Yield: 1 small loaf

In a 4-quart mixing bowl, dissolve the yeast in the water. Add the remaining ingredients, mixing the salt with the flour, and work them into a dough.

Turn the dough onto a lightly floured surface and knead for 6 to 7 minutes, until the dough is smooth, elastic, and somewhat glossy.

Return the dough to the mixing bowl and cover it with a towel. Let the dough rise in a warm (75° F.) place for 45 minutes, or until doubled in bulk.

Shape the dough into an oblong loaf. Set the loaf on a baking sheet that has been liberally dusted with cornmeal. Cover the loaf with a towel and let it rise again for 45 minutes.

Bake in a preheated 375° F. oven for 50 minutes, or until golden brown. Remove the loaf from the baking sheet at once and allow it to cool on a wire rack. After the bread has thoroughly cooled, cut it into small cubes and let them dry in a very slow oven (250° F.) for 45 to 50 minutes.

Peanut Delight Bread

This bread is a success with children. Serve it warm, with butter and honey.

1 cake yeast
2 cups warm (110° F.) water
4 teaspoons honey or sugar
2 eggs, at room temperature, lightly beaten
1/2 cup peanut butter
1 teaspoon salt
Approximately 6 cups unbleached all-purpose
   flour

Yield: 2 large round loaves

In a 6-quart mixing bowl, dissolve the yeast in the water. Add the remaining ingredients, mixing the salt with the flour, and work them into a dough.

Turn the dough onto a lightly floured surface and knead it for 6 to 7 minutes, until the dough is smooth, elastic, and somewhat glossy.

Return the dough to the mixing bowl and cover it with a towel. Let the dough rise in a warm (75° F.) place for 55 minutes, or until doubled in bulk.

Divide the dough into 2 equal halves and shape each piece into an oblong loaf. Set the loaves on a baking sheet that has been lightly greased with vegetable shortening. Cover the loaves with a towel and let them rise again for 55 minutes.

Bake in a preheated 375° F. oven for 50 minutes, or until golden brown. Remove the loaves from the baking sheet at once and allow them to cool on a wire rack.

6
Rolls

∞∞∞

In the Dutch language, rolls are called little breads. And, indeed, rolls can be made out of any bread recipe.

Most of the recipes for bread in this book make 2 loaves. Those same recipes will make 24 rolls (or 1 loaf plus 12 rolls). And for variation, you can mix into the dough any of the following: raisins, chopped nuts, grated rind of lemon or orange, chopped dried fruits, grated carrot, any sweet spice such as cinnamon or mace, or chopped fresh herbs.

The same principles that are outlined in the chapter on bread making basics apply to rolls. Just keep in mind that since rolls are small breads, the baking time should be reduced accordingly. Usually 20 to 25 minutes is sufficient baking time.

The baking sheet can be greased or dusted with cornmeal. I prefer to use a vegetable shortening for greasing. After many bakings, oil will make a baking sheet sticky and difficult to clean, while butter burns too easily. When you use a baking sheet, set the rolls 1 to 1 1/2 inches apart so that they don't stick together in the process of rising.

You can make an endless variety of shapes out of the same dough. The following are a few popular shapes.

Round Rolls. Divide the dough equally into small pieces. With lightly floured hands, shape the pieces into small balls. Flatten the balls slightly and set them on a greased baking sheet. Most of my recipes call for round rolls; however, you can choose to make the same rolls in a different shape.

Cloverleaf Rolls. After dividing the dough equally into small pieces for the rolls, cut each piece into thirds. Roll each piece into a little ball. Place 3 little balls into each greased cup of a muffin tin.

Braids. After dividing the dough equally into small pieces for the rolls, cut each piece into thirds. Roll each piece into a pencil-thin rope, 6 to 7 inches long. Weave the 3 ropes into a braid, and set the braids 1 inch apart on a greased baking sheet.

Pinwheel Rolls. With a rolling pin, roll out the dough to a rectangle 1/2 to 1 inch thick. Spread brown sugar and cinnamon or any other filling over the dough and roll up the rectangle as you would a jelly roll. Slice the roll 1 inch thick and place the slices flat on a greased baking sheet.

Dinner Rolls. Divide the dough into 12 to 18 equal-size pieces. Shape each piece into a round roll. Place the rolls on a greased baking sheet. Brush each roll with egg and sprinkle it with sesame seeds.

Bow Knots. Divide the dough equally into small pieces. Roll each piece into a pencil-thin rope about 10 inches long. Form a loose knot with each rope. Place them 1 inch apart on a greased baking sheet.

Parker House Rolls. With a rolling pin, roll out the dough to a flat sheet about 1/2 inch thick. Cut out the rolls with a floured 2 1/2-inch cookie cutter. Brush each roll with a little vegetable oil. Make a crease in the middle of each one and fold over so that the upper edge overlaps the lower edge a little and press the edges together gently. Place the rolls 1 inch apart on a greased baking sheet.

Bread Sticks. Divide the dough into small pieces. Roll each piece into a pencil-thin rope about 10 inches long. Brush each piece with egg white and sprinkle some sticks with sesame seeds, some with poppy seeds, and some with caraway. Set the sticks 1 inch apart on a greased baking sheet.

Snails. Divide the dough into small pieces. Roll each piece into a pencil-thin rope about 10 inches long. Make a swirl with each rope. Tuck the end under. Set the snails 1 inch apart on a greased baking sheet.

Sesame Hard Rolls

These crusty rolls taste somewhat like French bread. They are delicious spread with butter for dinner or with jam for breakfast.

Rolls

1 cake yeast
1 cup warm (110° F.) water
Approximately 3 cups unbleached all-purpose flour
1 teaspoon vegetable oil
2 egg whites, at room temperature
3/4 teaspoon salt

Glaze

1 egg white, at room temperature
Sesame seeds

Yield: 12 rolls

In a 4-quart mixing bowl, dissolve half the yeast in 1/2 cup of the water. Add 1/2 cup of the flour. Mix well. Let this ferment in a warm (75° F.) place for 3 1/2 hours. Then add the rest of the yeast and the water. Mix well. Add the remaining roll ingredients, mixing the salt with the flour, and work them into a dough.

Turn the dough out onto a lightly floured surface and knead it for 5 minutes, until the dough is smooth, elastic, and somewhat glossy.

Return the dough to the mixing bowl and cover with a towel. Let rise in a warm (75° F.) place for 50 minutes, or until doubled in bulk.

Divide the dough into 12 equal-size pieces and shape each piece into a 6-inch-long roll. Set 1 to 1 1/2 inches apart on a baking sheet that has been liberally dusted with cornmeal. Brush with egg white and sprinkle with sesame seeds. Let the rolls rise again for 45 minutes.

Bake in a preheated 400° F. oven for 15 to 20 minutes, or until golden brown. Cool on a wire rack.

Golden Rolls

These rolls taste very rich, and they are delicious with butter and cheese.

1 cake yeast
1 cup warm (110° F.) milk
2 teaspoons vegetable oil
1 tablespoon honey or sugar
3 egg yolks, at room temperature
3/4 teaspoon salt
Approximately 3 cups unbleached all-purpose
  flour

Yield: 12 rolls

In a 4-quart mixing bowl, dissolve the yeast in the milk. Add the remaining ingredients, mixing the salt with the flour, and work them into a dough.

Turn the dough out onto a lightly floured surface and knead it for 5 minutes, until the dough is smooth, elastic, and somewhat glossy.

Return the dough to the mixing bowl and cover it with a towel. Let the dough rise in a warm (75° F.) place for 50 minutes, or until doubled in bulk.

Divide the dough into 12 equal-size pieces and shape each piece into a round roll. Set the rolls 1 to 1 1/2 inches apart on a baking sheet that has been lightly greased with vegetable shortening. Cover the rolls with a towel and let them rise again for 45 minutes.

Bake in a preheated 375° F. oven for 20 minutes, or until golden brown. Remove the rolls from the baking sheet at once and allow them to cool on a wire rack.

Berliner Rolls

These delicious dinner rolls are easy to split for buttering. Known as Berliner Rolls in Germany, here they are called Parker House Rolls.

1 cake yeast
1 cup warm (110° F.) milk
2 teaspoons corn oil or any vegetable oil
1 teaspoon sorghum or sugar
3/4 teaspoon salt
Approximately 3 cups unbleached all-purpose
  flour

Yield: 10 rolls

In a 4-quart mixing bowl, dissolve the yeast in the milk. Add the remaining ingredients, mixing the salt with the flour, and work them into a dough.

Turn the dough out onto a lightly floured surface and knead it for 5 minutes, until the dough is smooth, elastic, and somewhat glossy.

Return the dough to the mixing bowl and cover with a towel. Let rise in a warm (75° F.) place for 45 minutes, or until doubled in bulk.

Roll out the dough about 1/4 inch thick. Cut out the rolls with a floured 2½-inch cookie cutter. Brush each with a little vegetable oil. Make a crease in the middle and fold over each roll so that the upper edge overlaps the lower edge a little, and press the edges together. Set 1 to 1 1/2 inches apart on a baking sheet that has been lightly greased with vegetable shortening. Cover with a towel and let rise again for 45 minutes.

Bake in a preheated 375° F. oven for 20 minutes, or until golden brown. Remove from the baking sheet and cool on a wire rack.

Sour Cream Rolls

∞∞∞

The sour cream gives these rolls a unique tangy flavor. They make a good accompaniment for stews and soups like borscht.

1 cake yeast
1 cup warm (110° F.) milk
1 teaspoon vegetable oil
2 teaspoons honey or sugar
2 eggs, at room temperature, lightly beaten
1/4 cup sour cream
Grated rind of 1 medium-size lemon
3/4 teaspoon salt
Approximately 3 cups unbleached all-purpose
    flour

Yield: 12 rolls

In a 4-quart mixing bowl, dissolve the yeast in the milk. Add the remaining ingredients, mixing the salt with the flour, and work them into a dough.

Turn the dough out onto a lightly floured surface and knead it for 5 minutes, until the dough is smooth, elastic, and somewhat glossy.

Return the dough to the mixing bowl and cover it with a towel. Let the dough rise in a warm (75° F.) place for 45 minutes, or until doubled in bulk.

Divide the dough into 12 equal-size pieces and shape each piece into a round roll. Set the rolls 1 to 1 1/2 inches apart on a baking sheet that has been lightly greased with vegetable shortening. Cover the rolls with a towel and let them rise again for 45 minutes.

Bake in a preheated 375° F. oven for 20 minutes, or until golden brown. Remove the rolls from the baking sheet at once and allow them to cool on a wire rack.

Potato Buns

These buns are rich and smooth tasting. They will stay fresh for several days, so you can bake them ahead of time for a dinner party.

1 cake yeast
1 cup warm (110° F.) milk
2 teaspoons vegetable oil
2 teaspoons sorghum or sugar
1 egg, at room temperature, lightly beaten
1 medium-size potato, boiled and mashed
3/4 teaspoon salt
Approximately 3 cups unbleached all-purpose flour

Yield: 12 rolls

In a 4-quart mixing bowl, dissolve the yeast in the milk. Add the remaining ingredients, mixing the salt with the flour, and work them into a dough.

Turn the dough out onto a lightly floured surface and knead it for 5 minutes, until the dough is smooth, elastic, and somewhat glossy.

Return the dough to the mixing bowl and cover it with a towel. Let the dough rise in a warm (75° F.) place for 45 minutes, or until doubled in bulk.

Divide the dough into 12 equal-size pieces and shape each piece into a round roll. Set the rolls 1 to 1 1/2 inches apart on a baking sheet that has been lightly greased with vegetable shortening. Cover the rolls with a towel and let them rise again for 45 minutes.

Bake in a preheated 375° F. oven for 20 minutes, or until golden brown. Remove the rolls from the baking sheet at once and allow them to cool on a wire rack.

Rye Rolls

Rye rolls are easier to make than to pronounce, at least for a Dutchman. These hearty rolls, with their satisfying rye flavor, go well with a bowl of soup. You can use either light or dark rye flour, but dark rye flour will give these rolls heartier flavor.

1 cake yeast
1 cup warm (110° F.) water
1 teaspoon vegetable oil
1 teaspoon molasses
1 teaspoon caraway seeds
3/4 teaspoon salt
1 cup rye flour
Approximately 2 cups unbleached all-purpose flour

Yield: 12 rolls

In a 4-quart mixing bowl, dissolve the yeast in the water. Add the remaining ingredients, mixing the salt with the flour, and work them into a dough.

Turn the dough out onto a lightly floured surface and knead it for 5 minutes, until the dough is smooth, elastic, and somewhat glossy.

Return the dough to the mixing bowl and cover it with a towel. Let the dough rise in a warm (75° F.) place for 45 minutes, or until doubled in bulk.

Divide the dough into 12 equal-size pieces and shape each piece into a round roll. Set the rolls 1 to 1 1/2 inches apart on a baking sheet that has been lightly greased with vegetable shortening. Cover the rolls with a towel and let them rise again for 45 minutes.

Bake in a preheated 375° F. oven for 20 minutes, or until golden brown. Remove the rolls from the baking sheet at once and allow them to cool on a wire rack.

Oatmeal Rolls

These rolls have a somewhat coarse texture and a distinctive oatmeal flavor. They are perfect for breakfast, spread with butter and jam.

1 cake yeast
1 cup warm (110° F.) milk
2 teaspoons vegetable oil
1 tablespoon honey or sugar
2 eggs, at room temperature, lightly beaten
1 cup raw rolled oats
Pinch mace
3/4 teaspoon salt
Approximately 2 cups unbleached all-purpose
   flour

Yield: 12 rolls

In a 4-quart mixing bowl, dissolve the yeast in the milk. Add the remaining ingredients, mixing the salt with the flour, and work them into a dough.

Turn the dough out onto a lightly floured surface and knead it for 5 minutes, until the dough is smooth, elastic, and somewhat glossy.

Return the dough to the mixing bowl and cover it with a towel. Let the dough rise in a warm (75° F.) place for 45 minutes, or until doubled in bulk.

Divide the dough into 12 equal-size pieces and shape each piece into a round roll. Set the rolls 1 to 1 1/2 inches apart on a baking sheet that has been lightly greased with vegetable shortening. Cover the rolls with a towel and let them rise again for 45 minutes.

Bake in a preheated 375° F. oven for 20 minutes, or until golden brown. Remove the rolls from the baking sheet at once and allow them to cool on a wire rack.

Bran Rolls

These rolls are a delicious way to add a little fiber to your diet. The bran gives them a slightly nutty flavor. The rolls are very good served warm with butter.

1 cake yeast
1 cup warm (110° F.) milk
1 teaspoon vegetable oil
2 teaspoons sorghum or honey
1 egg, at room temperature, lightly beaten
1/2 cup bran
3/4 teaspoon salt
Approximately 2 1/2 cups unbleached
   all-purpose flour

Yield: 12 rolls

In a 4-quart mixing bowl, dissolve the yeast in the milk. Add the remaining ingredients, mixing the salt with the flour, and work them into a dough.

Turn the dough out onto a lightly floured surface and knead it for 5 minutes, until the dough is smooth, elastic, and somewhat glossy.

Return the dough to the mixing bowl and cover it with a towel. Let the dough rise in a warm (75° F.) place for 45 minutes, or until doubled in bulk.

Divide the dough into 12 equal-size pieces and shape each piece into a round roll. Set the rolls 1 to 1 1/2 inches apart on a baking sheet that has been lightly greased with vegetable shortening. Cover the rolls with a towel and let them rise again for 45 minutes.

Bake in a preheated 375° F. oven for 20 minutes, or until golden brown. Remove the rolls from the baking sheet at once and allow them to cool on a wire rack.

Onion Rolls

There's nothing like a variety of dinner rolls on a dinner table to impress family and friends. These rolls are very flavorful and very good companions for a bowl of soup or stew.

1 cake yeast
1 cup warm (110° F.) milk
1 teaspoon vegetable oil
2 teaspoons finely chopped onion
3/4 teaspoon salt
Approximately 3 cups unbleached all-purpose
    flour

Yield: 12 rolls

In a 4-quart mixing bowl, dissolve the yeast in the milk. Add the remaining ingredients, mixing the salt with the flour, and work them into a dough.

Turn the dough out onto a lightly floured surface and knead it for 5 minutes, until the dough is smooth, elastic, and somewhat glossy.

Return the dough to the mixing bowl and cover it with a towel. Let the dough rise in a warm (75° F.) place for 45 minutes, or until doubled in bulk.

Divide the dough into 12 equal-size pieces and shape each piece into a round roll. Set the rolls 1 to 1 1/2 inches apart on a baking sheet that has been lightly greased with vegetable shortening. Cover the rolls with a towel and let them rise again for 45 minutes.

Bake in a preheated 375° F. oven for 20 minutes, or until golden brown. Remove the rolls from the baking sheet at once and allow them to cool on a wire rack.

Nordic Cheese Rolls

These cheese rolls are just right for a real smorgasbord. They are delicious with ham or kippered herring snacks and beer.

1 cake yeast
1 cup warm (110° F.) milk
1 teaspoon vegetable oil
1 teaspoon sorghum or sugar
1 egg, at room temperature, lightly beaten
1/2 cup grated sharp cheese
1/2 teaspoon caraway seeds
3/4 teaspoon salt
1/2 cup whole wheat flour
Approximately 2 1/2 cups unbleached
    all-purpose flour

Yield: 12 rolls

In a 4-quart mixing bowl, dissolve the yeast in the milk. Add the remaining ingredients, mixing the salt with the flours, and work them into a dough.

Turn the dough out onto a lightly floured surface and knead it for 5 minutes, until the dough is smooth, elastic, and somewhat glossy.

Return the dough to the mixing bowl and cover it with a towel. Let the dough rise in a warm (75° F.) place for 45 minutes, or until doubled in bulk.

Divide the dough into 12 equal-size pieces and shape each piece into a round roll. Set the rolls 1 to 1 1/2 inches apart on a baking sheet that has been lightly greased with vegetable shortening. Cover the rolls with a towel and let them rise again for 45 minutes.

Bake in a preheated 375° F. oven for 20 minutes, or until golden brown. Remove the rolls from the baking sheet at once and allow them to cool on a wire rack.

Bacon Rolls

These crusty bacon rolls have a piquant flavor.
They are the perfect accompaniment to a dish of
baked beans.

1 cake yeast
1 cup warm (110° F.) water
2 egg whites, at room temperature, lightly
  beaten
1 teaspoon chopped fresh parsley
5 strips bacon, fried crisp and crumbled
1/2 teaspoon salt
Approximately 3 cups unbleached all-purpose
  flour

Yield: 12 rolls

In a 4-quart mixing bowl, dissolve the yeast in the
water. Add the remaining ingredients, mixing the
salt with the flour, and work them into a dough.

Turn the dough out onto a lightly floured surface and knead it for 5 minutes, until the dough
is smooth, elastic, and somewhat glossy.

Return the dough to the mixing bowl and cover
it with a towel. Let the dough rise in a warm (75°
F.) place for 45 minutes, or until doubled in bulk.

Divide the dough into 12 equal-size pieces and
shape each into a round roll. Set the rolls 1 to 1
1/2 inches apart on a baking sheet that has been
lightly greased with vegetable shortening. Cover
the rolls with a towel and let them rise again for
45 minutes.

Bake in a preheated 375° F. oven for 20 minutes,
or until golden brown. Remove the rolls from the
baking sheet at once and allow them to cool on
a wire rack.

Luncheon Bread Sticks

These bread sticks are flavored by the different seeds with which they are glazed.

Bread Sticks

1 cake yeast
1 cup warm (110° F.) milk
1 teaspoon corn oil or other vegetable oil
2 teaspoons honey or sugar
3/4 teaspoon salt
Approximately 3 cups unbleached all-purpose
  flour

Glaze

1 egg white, at room temperature, lightly beaten
Sesame, poppy, and/or caraway seeds

Yield: 12 rolls

In a 4-quart mixing bowl, dissolve the yeast in the milk. Add the remaining bread stick ingredients, mixing the salt with the flour, and work them into a dough.

Turn the dough out onto a lightly floured surface and knead it for 5 minutes, until the dough is smooth, elastic, and somewhat glossy.

Return the dough to the mixing bowl and cover with a towel. Let rise in a warm (75° F.) place for 45 minutes, or until doubled in bulk.

Divide the dough into 12 equal-size pieces and shape each into a pencil-thin rope about 10 inches long. Brush with the egg white and sprinkle some with sesame seeds, some with poppy seeds, and some with caraway and poppy seeds. Set 1 to 1 1/2 inches apart on a baking sheet that has been lightly greased with vegetable shortening. Cover with a towel and let them rise again for 45 minutes.

Bake in a preheated 375° F. oven for 20 minutes, or until golden brown. Remove from the baking sheet at once and cool on a wire rack.

Dutch Bestelle (Bagels)

Bagels, the Jewish rolls, are fast becoming Americanized, like pizza. Traditionally they are eaten with cream cheese and lox, but, as Americans have found out, they are good with cold cuts, cheese, and a variety of fillings.

Bagel

1 cake yeast
2 cups warm (110° F.) water
Approximately 6 cups unbleached all-purpose flour
4 teaspoons vegetable oil
4 teaspoons honey or sugar
2 eggs, at room temperature, lightly beaten
1 teaspoon salt

Glaze (optional)

Egg white, at room temperature, lightly beaten
Sesame or poppy seeds, or finely chopped onion

Yield: 24 bagels

In a 6-quart mixing bowl, dissolve half the yeast in 1 cup of the water. Add 1 cup of the flour. Mix well. Let this ferment in a warm place (75° F.) for 3 1/2 hours. Then add the rest of the yeast and the water. Add the remaining bagel ingredients, mixing the salt with the remaining flour, and work them into a dough.

Turn the dough out onto a lightly floured surface and knead it for 6 to 7 minutes, until the dough is smooth, elastic, and somewhat glossy.

Return the dough to the mixing bowl and cover it with a towel. Let the dough rise in a warm (75° F.) place for 45 minutes, or until doubled in bulk.

Divide the dough into 2 equal halves and shape each half into a round loaf. Cover the loaves with a towel and let them rise for 30 minutes. Then punch down each loaf. Divide each loaf into 12 equal-size pieces. Shape each piece into a round ball. Punch a hole in the center of each with your finger. Have a pan of boiling water ready.

Drop each bagel into the boiling water. Do this

a few at a time, so as not to crowd them in the pan.
After they come to the top of the boiling water,
boil them for 2 minutes. Then turn them over and
cook the other side for 2 minutes. Then, remove
them and place them on a greased baking sheet.
Repeat this until you have all the bagels boiled and
placed on the baking sheet. For variety, you can
brush each bagel with the egg white before baking. You can also sprinkle them with sesame seeds,
poppy seeds, or finely chopped onions after brush-
ing them with the egg white.

Bake in a preheated 375° F. oven for 30 minutes,
or until golden brown. Remove the bagels from the
baking sheet at once and allow them to cool on
a wire rack.

Cottage Cheese Rolls

These zesty rolls are very popular in South Holland for Sunday morning breakfast.

Rolls

1 cake yeast
1 cup warm (110° F.) milk
2 teaspoons vegetable oil
2 teaspoons honey
1 egg, at room temperature, lightly beaten
Grated rind of 1 medium-size lemon
3/4 teaspoon salt
Approximately 3 cups unbleached all-purpose
   flour

Filling

1/2 cup cottage cheese
1/2 cup honey
Pinch salt
Grated rind of 1 medium-size lemon
1/2 cup chopped dried currants

Yield: 12 rolls

In a 4-quart mixing bowl, dissolve the yeast in the milk. Add the remaining roll ingredients, mixing the salt with the flour, and work them into a dough.

Turn the dough out onto a lightly floured surface and knead it for 5 minutes, until the dough is smooth, elastic, and somewhat glossy.

Return the dough to the mixing bowl and cover with a towel. Let rise in a warm (75° F.) place for 45 minutes, or until doubled in bulk.

Divide the dough into 12 equal-size pieces and shape each into a round roll. Set 1 to 1 1/2 inches apart on a baking sheet that has been lightly greased with vegetable shortening. Let the rolls rise for 10 minutes. Meanwhile, mix the ingredients for the filling. Then press 3 fingers into each roll to make a deep indentation. Place 1/2 teaspoon of filling into each indentation. Let rise again for 45 minutes.

Bake in a preheated 375° F. oven for 20 minutes, or until golden brown. Remove from the baking sheet and cool on a wire rack.

Orange Rolls

These somewhat sweet, citrus-flavored rolls make the perfect accompaniment for an afternoon tea. Serve warm, with butter and honey or jam.

1 cake yeast
1 cup warm (110° F.) milk
Grated rind of 1 medium-size orange
2 teaspoons vegetable oil
1 tablespoon honey or sugar
2 eggs, at room temperature, lightly beaten
2 teaspoons orange marmalade
3/4 teaspoon salt
Approximately 3 cups unbleached all-purpose
  flour

Yield: 12 rolls

In a 4-quart mixing bowl, dissolve the yeast in the milk. Add the remaining ingredients, mixing the salt with the flour, and work them into a dough.

Turn the dough out onto a lightly floured surface and knead it for 5 minutes, until the dough is smooth, elastic, and somewhat glossy.

Return the dough to the mixing bowl and cover it with a towel. Let the dough rise in a warm (75° F.) place for 45 minutes, or until doubled in bulk.

Divide the dough into 12 equal-size pieces and shape each piece into a round roll. Set the rolls 1 to 1 1/2 inches apart on a baking sheet that has been lightly greased with vegetable shortening. Cover the rolls with a towel and let them rise again for 45 minutes.

Bake in a preheated 375° F. oven for 20 minutes, or until golden brown. Remove the rolls from the baking sheet at once and allow them to cool on a wire rack.

Carrot Rolls

Moist and soft on the inside and not overly sweet, these rolls make a welcome addition to a breakfast tray.

1 cake yeast
1 cup warm (110° F.) milk
1 teaspoon corn or other vegetable oil
1 tablespoon honey or sugar
2 egg yolks, at room temperature
1/2 cup grated carrots
Pinch cinnamon
3/4 teaspoon salt
Approximately 3 cups unbleached all-purpose flour

Yield: 12 rolls

In a 4-quart mixing bowl, dissolve the yeast in the milk. Add the remaining ingredients, mixing the salt with the flour, and work them into a dough.

Turn the dough out onto a lightly floured surface and knead it for 5 minutes, until the dough is smooth, elastic, and somewhat glossy.

Return the dough to the mixing bowl and cover it with a towel. Let the dough rise in a warm (75° F.) place for 45 minutes, or until doubled in bulk.

Divide the dough into 12 equal-size pieces and shape each piece into a round roll. Set the rolls 1 to 1 1/2 inches apart on a baking sheet that has been lightly greased with vegetable shortening. Cover the rolls with a towel and let them rise again for 45 minutes.

Bake in a preheated 375° F. oven for 20 minutes, or until golden brown. Remove the rolls from the baking sheet at once and allow them to cool on a wire rack.

Rum Rolls

The dark rum gives these rolls a unique flavor. They are pleasantly sweet and make a good choice for an afternoon coffee or tea.

1 cake yeast
1 cup warm (110° F.) milk
1 teaspoon corn or other vegetable oil
1 tablespoon honey or sugar
2 eggs, at room temperature, lightly beaten
1/4 cup dark rum
1 teaspoon pure vanilla extract
3/4 teaspoon salt
Approximately 3 cups unbleached all-purpose
    flour

Yield: 12 rolls

In a 4-quart mixing bowl, dissolve the yeast in the milk. Add the remaining ingredients, mixing the salt with the flour, and work them into a dough.

Turn the dough out onto a lightly floured surface and knead it for 5 minutes, until the dough is smooth, elastic, and somewhat glossy.

Return the dough to the mixing bowl and cover it with a towel. Let the dough rise in a warm (75° F.) place for 45 minutes, or until doubled in bulk.

Divide the dough into 12 equal-size pieces and shape each piece into a round roll. Set the rolls 1 to 1 1/2 inches apart on a baking sheet that has been lightly greased with vegetable shortening. Cover the rolls with a towel and let them rise again for 45 minutes.

Bake in a preheated 375° F. oven for 20 minutes, or until golden brown. Remove the rolls from the baking sheet at once and allow them to cool on a wire rack.

Crumb Rolls

Rolls

1 cake yeast
1 cup warm (110° F.) milk
2 teaspoons vegetable oil
1 tablespoon honey or sugar
1 egg, at room temperature, lightly beaten
Pinch mace
3/4 teaspoon salt
Approximately 3 cups unbleached all-purpose
   flour

Glaze

1 egg, at room temperature, lightly beaten

Crumb Topping

1/2 cup butter, at room temperature
1/2 cup brown sugar
1/2 teaspoon cinnamon
Pinch ground cloves
1/2 cup unbleached all-purpose flour

Yield: 12 rolls

In a 4-quart mixing bowl, dissolve the yeast in the milk. Add the remaining roll ingredients, mixing the salt with the flour, and work them into a dough.

Turn the dough out onto a lightly floured surface and knead it for 5 minutes, until the dough is smooth, elastic, and somewhat glossy.

Return the dough to the mixing bowl and cover with a towel. Let rise in a warm (75° F.) place for 45 minutes, or until doubled in bulk.

Divide the dough into 12 equal-size pieces and shape each into a round roll. Press each roll flat, and brush with the lightly beaten egg.

Cream together the butter and brown sugar. Add the spices and flour, mixing it into a crumbly mixture. Sprinkle over the rolls.

Set the rolls 1 to 1 1/2 inches apart on a baking sheet that has been lightly greased with vegetable shortening. Let them rise again for 50 minutes.

Bake in a preheated 350° F. oven for 25 to 30 minutes, or until golden brown. Remove the rolls from the baking sheet at once and allow them to cool on a wire rack.

Cinnamon Rolls

∞∞

Cinnamon rolls are popular in many countries. There is nothing to compare with the aroma of these rolls baking.

Rolls

1 cake yeast
1 cup of warm (110° F.) milk
2 teaspoons vegetable oil
1 tablespoon honey or sugar
2 eggs, at room temperature, lightly beaten
1/2 cup raisins
1/2 cup chopped pecans
3/4 teaspoon salt
Approximately 3 cups unbleached all-purpose
   flour

Filling

1 teaspoon melted butter
3/4 cup brown sugar
1 teaspoon cinnamon

Yield: 12 rolls

In a 4-quart mixing bowl, dissolve the yeast in the milk. Add the remaining ingredients, mixing the salt with the flour, and work them into a dough.

Turn the dough out onto a lightly floured surface and knead it for 5 minutes, until the dough is smooth, elastic, and somewhat glossy.

Return the dough to the mixing bowl and cover with a towel. Let rise in a warm (75° F.) place for 50 minutes, or until doubled in bulk.

Roll the dough flat, about 1/2 inch thick. Brush with the melted butter. Mix together the brown sugar and cinnamon and sprinkle generously over the dough. Roll up the dough as you would a jelly roll. With a sharp knife, cut 12 even slices, about 3/4 inch to 1 inch thick. Set the slices flat, 1 to 1 1/2 inches apart, on a baking sheet that has been lightly greased with vegetable shortening. Cover with a towel and let rise again for 45 minutes.

Bake in a preheated 350° F. oven for 25 minutes, or until golden brown. Remove the rolls from the baking sheet at once and allow them to cool on a wire rack.

Dutch Apple Rolls

These rolls have a delicious apple filling. They are a real Dutch treat you won't mind sharing with friends and family.

Rolls

1 cake yeast
1 cup warm (110° F.) milk
2 teaspoons vegetable oil
1 tablespoon sorghum or sugar
1 egg, at room temperature, lightly beaten
3/4 teaspoon salt
Approximately 3 cups unbleached all-purpose flour

Filling

1 apple, peeled and chopped
1 tablespoon brown sugar
1/2 teaspoon cinnamon

Yield: 12 rolls

In a 4-quart mixing bowl, dissolve the yeast in the milk. Add the remaining ingredients, mixing the salt with the flour, and work them into a dough.

Turn the dough out onto a lightly floured surface and knead it for 5 minutes, until the dough is smooth, elastic, and somewhat glossy.

Return the dough to the mixing bowl and cover with a towel. Let rise in a warm (75° F.) place for 50 minutes, or until doubled in bulk.

Roll the dough flat, about 1/2 inch thick. Brush with the melted butter. Combine the filling ingredients and mix well. Spread over the dough. Roll up the dough as you would a jelly roll. With a sharp knife, cut into 3/4-inch slices. Set the slices flat, 1 to 1 1/2 inches apart, on a baking sheet that has been lightly greased with vegetable shortening. Cover with a towel and let rise again for 45 minutes.

Bake in a preheated 375° F. oven for 25 minutes, or until golden brown. Remove the rolls from the baking sheet at once and allow them to cool on a wire rack.

Berliner Ketle Kuchen

These German rolls are very similar to American jelly doughnuts, without the jelly. They are light and yet very filling. These rolls are best when served warm.

1 cake yeast
1 cup warm (110° F.) milk
2 teaspoons sorghum or sugar
1 egg, at room temperature, lightly beaten
1 teaspoon pure vanilla extract
3/4 teaspoon salt
Approximately 3 cups unbleached all-purpose flour
Oil for deep frying
Cinnamon sugar

Yield: 12 rolls

In a 4-quart mixing bowl, dissolve the yeast in the milk. Add the sorghum or sugar, egg, and vanilla. Mix the salt with the flour and add, working it into a dough.

Turn the dough out onto a lightly floured surface and knead it for 5 minutes, until the dough is smooth, elastic, and somewhat glossy.

Return the dough to the mixing bowl and cover it with a towel. Let the dough rise in a warm (75° F.) place for 1 hour, or until doubled in bulk.

Divide the dough into 12 equal-size pieces and shape each piece into a round roll. Set the rolls on a lightly floured surface, cover them with a towel, and let them rise for 20 minutes.

Preheat the oil in a deep fryer to 375° F. Drop each roll into the hot oil, being careful not to overcrowd the rolls in the fryer. Cook each roll for 2 minutes on one side, then turn them over and cook for another 2 minutes, or until golden brown. Remove them with a slotted spoon, drain on paper towels, and sprinkle with cinnamon sugar.

Index

175

Printed in the United States
By Bookmasters